P9-AGA-555

# DATE DUE

| APR 23 | | | |
|--------|--|--|--|
| | | | |
| | | | |
| | | | |
| | | | |
| | | | |
| | | | |
| | | | |
| | | | |
| | | | |
| | | | |
| | | | |
| | | | |
| | | | |
| | | | |
| | | | |
| | | | Demco |
| | | | |

*Twayne's United States Authors Series*

Sylvia E. Bowman, *Editor*

INDIANA UNIVERSITY

*James Whitcomb Riley*

(TUSAS) 159

# James Whitcomb Riley

By PETER REVELL

University College, Cardiff

TWAYNE PUBLISHERS

A DIVISION OF G. K. HALL & CO., BOSTON

FOR FRANCESS

# Contents

# Preface

The verse and prose of James Whitcomb Riley have not previously received any extended critical examination, and even as brief a study as this one is largely pioneer work. This is true not only in that the ground is so far untrodden but also that no adequate methodology has been developed by contemporary critics for the discussion of popular verse of this order. There are no problems of interpretation, since Riley wrote from the first with the most general of readers in mind and sought to make his meanings transparently clear. There can also be no analysis of development, in the normally accepted sense of this term. Once he had found a style, or styles, which could command wide public acceptance, Riley was wise enough, commercially speaking, to content himself with repeating a successful pattern.

The most fruitful approach to the work of a popular artist appears to be the stylistic one. The sociological approach, which might provide some useful insights, tends always to lead interest away from the text itself and to overload the discussion with social history. My aim throughout this study has been to concentrate on the verse and prose, to discover in these the sources from which Riley created his money-making poetic styles, and to analyze the ways in which the poet adapted his sources in order to achieve popular acceptance. As a basis for discussion I have provided some preliminary observations on the place of the popular writer in literature and a biographical summary intended to give the reader some notion of the background from which Riley sprang; the type of audience for which he began to write; and the methods by which, as a writer and as a successful agent for his wares, he sought to achieve a national audience.

Although Riley is best known today as a writer of dialect verse, he had two identities as a popular poet, which I have called "the Victorian poet" and "the Hoosier poet." In the first, he writes poems of love, of art, of bereavement and sorrow in a debased amalgam of the styles of the acceptedly correct literary artists of nineteenth-century England and America. In the second, he writes ostensibly for a humbler audience, and he celebrates the commonplaces of life in the language of plain people. The real secret of his popular success is that his work in dialect, like that of some of his predecessors in the American dialect tradition, ultimately proved acceptable to all tastes, to all classes in all parts of America; and the Hoosier became a nationally recognizable type. Riley's work as a children's poet, which calls for separate consideration, draws on both his identities. As a writer of dialect verse, he created an original blend of the dialect and the pastoral traditions which I have given special attention in the chapter on the Middle Western pastoral.

The question why a popular writer should have achieved widespread acceptance how and when he did is of particular interest from the literary historical point of view. I have sought to bear this question in mind throughout the detailed discussion of Riley's work and to summarize my conclusions in the last two chapters. A comprehensive analysis of all the poems and prose sketches of this prolific writer would not be possible in a study of this length, nor would it be profitable in the discussion of a writer so given to repeating his earlier successes. I have preferred to limit discussion to the most popular items and to representative examples of the less popular.

In preparing this study, my chief debt, as the notes and references will testify, has been to Riley's biographers, Marcus Dickey and Richard Crowder, for the wealth of information they provide on the circumstances in which his work was done. I also want to thank the curators and guides of the two Riley homes, at Lockerbie Street, Indianapolis and Greenfield, Indiana, for helping me to an understanding of the regional setting.

PETER REVELL

Cardiff, Wales

# Acknowledgments

The author wishes to thank the publishers and holders of copy‑right named below for permission to use quotations:

From *The Biographical Edition of the Complete Works of James Whitcomb Riley,* copyright 1913 by James Whitcomb Riley, 1940 by Lesley Payne, Elizabeth Eitel Miesse and Ed‑mund H. Eitel. Reprinted by permission of the publishers, The Bobbs-Merrill Company, Inc.

From *The Letters of James Whitcomb Riley,* copyright 1930 by Mary Riley Payne, Elizabeth Eitel Miesse and Edmund H. Eitel. Copyright renewed 1958 by Lesley Payne, Elizabeth Eitel Miesse and Edmund H. Eitel. Reprinted by permission of the publishers, The Bobbs-Merrill Company, Inc.

From the *Yale Literary Magazine,* February 1907; "Editor's Table," by Sinclair Lewis. Copyright, the Estate of Sinclair Lewis.

From *Main Street,* by Sinclair Lewis. Reprinted by permission of the publishers, Harcourt, Brace & World, Inc.

From *The New Basic History of the United States,* by Charles A. and Mary R. Beard. Copyright © 1944, 1960 by Doubleday & Company, Inc. Reprinted by permission of the publisher.

# Chronology

1849    James Whitcomb Riley, born October 7, at Greenfield, Indiana ("a village of 300 inhabitants" in 1844), the son of Reuben Riley, a lawyer and member of the state legislature.

1855–  Educated sporadically at home by his mother and sisters
1869    and at various local tuition-supported schools.

1870    Greenfield Academy, Greenfield's first public school opened; Riley listed as a pupil, but left at end of first term.

1870–  Brief experiences as a clerk in a shoe store, a Bible sales-
1871    man, and a house painter. First poem published, "The Same Old Story Told Again," in the *Greenfield Commercial*, Sept. 7, 1870. A few other poems were published in local small-town newspapers in the period 1870–76.

1871    Set up shop as a signpainter.

1872–  Toured with a patent-medicine selling show, as a minstrel
1874    and jingle-writer, and with the Graphic Company, an itinerant group of signpainters. The tours, through Indiana, Ohio, and Illinois, were based in Anderson, Indiana.

1874    First solo appearance as a recitation artist at Monrovia, Indiana, summer.

1875    Solo tour of the towns of central Indiana as a "humorist and recitationist." "A Destiny" published April 10 in *Hearth and Home* (New York).

1875–  Entered his father's law office but left after one year.
1876

1876    Toured with the Wizard Oil Company, another patent-medicine troupe, as an entertainer. Early versions of some of his poems were written on these tours to entertain the public. Continued to give readings in churches and schoolhouses of small towns through the next two years.

1877    January 10: First poem published in the *Indianapolis Journal*. April–August: Employed as assistant to the editor of the *Anderson Democrat,* contributing poems, humorous sketches, parodies, and advertising jingles. August 2: "Leonainie," published in the *Kokomo Dispatch* as a newly discovered work of Poe, starts the "Leonainie" hoax. Exposed by a rival newspaper, August 30.

1878–
1880    Numerous contributions to the *Indianapolis Journal, Kokomo Tribune,* and *Indianapolis Saturday Herald.* Many of these reprinted in newspapers across the country.

1879    November: Began regular employment with the *Indianapolis Journal* as the paper's resident poet and humorist. Continued in this capacity until 1888. Permanent resident of Indianapolis from this date.

1881    Friendship with Joel Chandler Harris began, ending with Harris's death in 1908.

1882    January: His first reading in Boston, at Tremont Temple, as part of a Redpath Lyceum Bureau reading tour; a great success with public and critics. Met Longfellow. Riley's reading tours are repeated almost every year from this date until 1903. June 17: First of the "Benjamin F. Johnson of Boone" poems published in *Indianapolis Journal.*

1883    *The Old Swimmin'-Hole, and 'Leven More Poems* published in Cincinnati and Indianapolis. *Century Magazine* bought poem "Nothin' to Say," but did not publish it until August, 1887.

1885    *The Boss Girl* (prose sketches) published.

1886    First series of readings with Bill Nye.

1887    Invited to read at Chickering Hall, New York, November 28 and 29, under auspices of the International Copyright League. This success with the Eastern establishment marked complete national acceptance by public and critics. *Afterwhiles* published.

1888    Second appearance at Chickering Hall, with Bill Nye and G. W. Cable. *Old-Fashioned Roses* published by Longmans (first publication in England). *Nye and Riley's Railway Guide* (humorous poems and sketches) published in Chicago. *Pipes o' Pan at Zekesbury* published in Indianapolis. Ceased regular employment with *Indianapolis Journal.*

1890    Last reading with Nye. *Rhymes of Childhood* published.

1891    Visited Scotland and England. Irving gave a dinner in his honor at the Savoy. *The Flying Islands of The Night.*

## Chronology

1892  *Green Fields and Running Brooks*. Reading tour in the West Coast region.

1893  *Poems Here at Home* published by Century Company, New York (first book published in the East). Began residence at 26 (now 528) Lockerbie Street, Indianapolis, as a permanent paying guest of Major Charles L. Holstein. Bought the old homestead at Greenfield, which became his summer residence. Met Kipling in New York.

1894  *Armazindy*.

1896  *A Child-World* published in Indianapolis, and by Longmans in London. Reading tour in the Southwest.

1897  *Rubaiyat of Doc Sifers* published by Century Company, New York. Charles Scribner's Sons, New York, published the first volume of the Homestead edition.

1898  First poems published in *Atlantic Monthly*. Reading tour of the South.

1900  *Home-Folks*.

1902  Honorary M.A. from Yale University. *The Book of Joyous Children*.

1903  Last reading tour. *His Pa's Romance*. Portrait by J. S. Sargent.

1904  Honorary Doctor of Letters, University of Philadelphia.

1906  Trip to Mexico City.

1907  Honorary Doctor of Laws, Indiana University. *Morning* published.

1908  Elected to National Institute of Arts and Letters.

1910  October 7th observed as "Riley Day" in Indiana schools.

1911  Elected to American Academy of Arts and Letters. *The Lockerbie Book*, collection of the nondialect poems.

1913  Biographical edition, collected verse and prose, published.

1915  National Commissioner of Education directed "Riley Day" to be observed at all schools in the United States.

1916  *The Hoosier Book*, collection of the dialect verse. Died, July 22.

1930  *Letters of James Whitcomb Riley* published.

James Whitcomb Riley

### CHAPTER 1

# The Popular Poet

IN HIS study of John Greenleaf Whittier,[1] Lewis Leary lists James Whitcomb Riley—along with Longfellow, Holmes, and Whittier—as one of the great "short-order cooks" of literature. The implication is that these poets are expert in the preparation of simple, undemanding concoctions that are acceptable to all and sundry and that provide a form of temporary mental sustenance forgotten as soon as consumed. This description applies with special justice to Riley, since for eleven years, and during all of his most productive decade, the years 1876 to 1886, he was a newspaper writer, contributing verse and prose, both "comic" and "serious," on demand and writing essentially for a day-to-day public. It would appear, therefore, that some form of introductory apologia and justification is called for in undertaking the study of what is, for all its six collected volumes and one thousand and forty-four poems, so comparatively lightweight an *oeuvre*. This justification must also include a consideration of the special problems involved in the criticism of minor poetry and the methodology to be employed in the present study.

The first thing to be established about the work of James Whitcomb Riley is its extraordinary popularity during the author's lifetime. When Hamlin Garland interviewed Riley for *McClure's Magazine* in 1894, the poet, "Although living so simply . . . confessed . . . somewhat shamefacedly (yet with boyish pride), that his royalties that year were greater than those of any other American poet except Longfellow. In addition to the income from his books, he was in constant demand as a reader." [2] When *An Old Sweetheart of Mine* was published in a separate, illustrated volume in 1902, having first appeared in the *Indianapolis Journal* for March 12, 1877, and been collected in numerous Riley books before 1902, it was estimated that the poem, one of eighteen four-line stanzas, had brought him five hundred dollars a word.[3]

## I  *Universal Acceptance*

The extraordinary nature of Riley's popularity lies not merely in its commercially realizable value but in the fact that it was accomplished almost with no dissenting voice. It might be argued that this is a result of the customary indifference of serious critics to the popular literary idols of their day, that we will not today find W. H. Auden dissenting from the popular valuation of Agatha Christie, or (on another level) Granville Hicks deploring the commercial success of *Oklahoma*. It seems clear, however, that there is not in these examples any question of a clear line of demarcation between a "popular" art and an "élite" art, such as Roy Harvey Pearce proposes in his discussion of late nineteenth-century American poetry.[4] The great commercial success of the modern authors of light fiction and light revue appears to lie rather in their ability to provide a form of entertainment acceptable to all classes and all levels of artistic appreciation.

The points of difference between the "serious artist" and the "popular writer" are, however, increasingly hard to establish as the relationship of writer and audience changes. While we may have no doubt on which side of the fence a Marianne Moore or a Faith Baldwin belongs, there is less certainty about a John O'Hara or a Kingsley Amis. The work of such writers of entertainment fiction as Dashiell Hammett and Raymond Chandler has, for some critics, begun to acquire importance as social commentary and significant form in such a way as to merit the same consideration as does serious fiction. While some writers (Graham Greene, T. S. Eliot) consciously separate their serious from their light work, others (Arthur Miller, John Osborne) work diligently at eliminating the distinction and at rendering the content of their serious work acceptable in terms of the media of mass entertainment.

In considering the work of James Whitcomb Riley, we are clearly involved with the question of "popular" and "élite" art—or with a "popular" art which was also acceptable to an élite audience—at a time which may be regarded as the beginning of the modern period of mass audiences and the manipulation of popular taste by publishing techniques. It was also a time when literary criticism in the United States was half-baked, provincial, and capricious. There were no academic critics capable of distinguishing the emerging forms of the American literary tradition and no critical press with a view beyond the fashion of the day.

Riley was, to his age, the entertainer par excellence; and, in the last twenty years of his life, his work and his personality were exploited with great commercial acumen—but he was far more than a mere entertainer. He expressed the spirit of the era in a way which made him increasingly "beloved" by that age, and he expressed for it the same qualities of universal humanity, of solicitude and respect for the poor and the meek, which have made Robert Burns and Charles Dickens especially "beloved" by readers who look for the affirmation of universal human values in their literature. It was not for nothing that Burns and Dickens, together with Longfellow, were Riley's models throughout his career and that he sought especially to recreate their spirit in his work.

By the time of Riley's appearances at public readings in Boston and New York in the 1880's, he had already won a considerable following in the Middle West as a newspaper writer of wholesome, entertaining verse and prose. His acceptance on a national level depended upon his success in the East. His first appearance at Tremont Temple, Boston, in January, 1882, was a popular success with the audience; and Riley was made much of by Boston literary society; invited to the anniversary banquet of the Papyrus Club, where he met William Dean Howells and Thomas Bailey Aldrich; taken to the Craigie House to meet Longfellow, and on "a glorious yacht ride." [5] "I'm destined to meet every literary potentate of the town—and on an equality too. Just think of it!" [6] he wrote home enthusiastically to a friend in Indianapolis. Boston was to do the same for Matthew Arnold the following year.

The gains of this promising beginning were quickly consolidated. The twelve poems of the "Benjamin F. Johnson of Boone" series were published at intervals during 1882 in the *Indianapolis Journal* and as Riley's first book the following year, when they won the respectful attention of Mark Twain and Joel Chandler Harris, among others. By 1887, Riley's stock in the East had steadily grown. The *Century Magazine* had published one poem, "In Swimming Time," in September, 1883, and had accepted another ("Nothin' to Say," which subsequently became a popular favorite) in the same year but did not publish it until August, 1887.

At this time, the *Century Magazine* was a leading literary journal. Frank Luther Mott states that "at the beginning of the twenty-year period 1885–1905, the leaders in the field of national illustrated monthlies devoted to the publication of literary miscellany were two New York magazines, *Harper's* and the *Century*; and at the end of the period, though more or less battered by competition of many kinds, these two, with the addition of *Scribner's*, were still leaders in what they liked to call the 'quality' magazine class." [7]

In February, 1887, however, Riley had won with "The Old Man and Jim" the unqualified approval of the *Century's* sub-editor, Robert Underwood Johnson. "You have hit the bull's eye this time," Johnson had written. "The thing is a poem clean through. I would give a hundred dollars to have written it." It was Johnson who invited Riley to read at Chickering Hall, New York, on November 28, 1887, under the auspices of the International Copyright League, and in the distinguished company of George William Curtis, Mark Twain, George Washington Cable, W. D. Howells, Frank R. Stockton, Charles Dudley Warner, Edward Eggleston, and Thomas Nelson Page, with James Russell Lowell presiding. Riley read on the twenty-eighth, was a great success with the audience, and was invited to appear again for the second day's readings. Lowell, in introducing Riley on the second night, said he had been "almost a stranger to his poems," had sat up to read them after the first night's reading, and had "been so impressed with the tenderness and beauty" of what he had read, "so much of high worth and tender quality," that he could "say of [his] own knowledge that you are to have the pleasure of listening to a true poet." [8]

## II  *The New Audience*

Professor Pearce has commented on Lowell's attitude to the popular audience for poetry. As early as 1848, Lowell had written to C. F. Briggs: "I am the first poet who has endeavoured to express the American idea and I shall be popular by and by." In Pearce's view, he "could not avoid seeing that Poe, Emerson and Whitman were as much rejected by American culture as they—to a degree, in spite of themselves—rejected it. What could be gained in a society in which poets were at odds with the people? Lowell trimmed his sails before the winds of social change and came gradually to be the spokesman for a middle way of culture, in which the best of everything was to be cut down to the size of a people—an entirely new kind of popular audience—not yet up to the demands of the best." [9]

Riley had arrived at the "middle way of culture," no less surely and no less "successfully," from the other direction by elevating—rendering acceptable to persons of education—the lowly products of the newspaper muse. The fact that he had done so with conspicuous success in the medium of dialect verse may have appeared especially relevant to Lowell, who had himself first won a large audience with the dialect poems of the *Biglow Papers*. Although the particular relation of the *Biglow Papers* and Riley's dialect poems will be discussed later, my concern for the moment is to establish that, by the late 1880's, Riley had won himself the respect and praise of the highest literary authorities in America. The chorus of praise, in which Lowell's tribute sounds the first note, was to continue undiminished until Riley's death.

When *Rhymes of Childhood* was published in 1890, Howells wrote in *Harper's Magazine* that the book "takes itself quite out of the category of ordinary verse and refuses to be judged by the usual criterions. . . . What [the poet] has said of very common aspects of life has endeared him to the public. You feel, in reading his verse, that here is one of the honestest souls that ever uttered itself in that way." [10] Riley's depiction of "poor dear real life" always made more of its "foolish face" than its ugly face, but Howells' praise cannot be thus explained away. John Hay and Twain wrote letters of thanks to the poet for this book. "Thanks a thousand, thousand times," wrote Twain, "for the charming book which laments my own lost youth for me as no words of mine could do." [11] Kipling's poem "To J. W. R." was a tribute of thanks to Riley for this same volume.

Perhaps the feelings of public and critics about the achievement of the poet were most clearly stated in the public orator's address at the award of the honorary master of arts degree to Riley at Yale in 1902: "This Hoosier has achieved the name, the fame, and the still more enviable influence of a national poet. His hundreds of thousands of readers came to love him as Whittier and Longfellow were loved. The rustic voices of his dialect have revealed Theocritan and Sicilian shepherds in our Indiana." [12] The endorsements of mass appeal, traditional soundness, and educated approval are all sounded in this tribute, and the accolade of Presidential acclaim was to come to Riley, as it came to Robert Frost, late in life, when Woodrow Wilson sent warm greetings and regrets that he could not be present at the Riley birthday celebrations in 1915, and stated: "I wish that I might be present to render my tribute of affectionate appreciation to him for the many pleasures he has given me, along with the rest of the great body of readers of English." [13]

Having established the kind and the degree of Riley's fame and popularity, it is necessary to give some attention to biographical matters in order to determine the means by which Riley won his popular audience. This popularity was achieved entirely on his own initiative, with none of the machinery employed by the publisher-entrepreneur of today, though this last was abundantly in evidence in the later years of Riley's career. There was, of course, nothing new, by the 1870's and 1880's, about the idea of making a living by the practice of the art of writing. Scott, Dickens, and Twain are only the more famous examples of the many nineteenth-century writers who made a business career of their art. Riley is, however, an outstanding early instance of the commercial writer in the modern sense,[14] one who found a field which was sure of abundant return, and worked it without ceasing. The consideration of the steps by which he arrived at this state says much about the reading public of his day and about the conditions under which an aspiring poet could obtain a hearing and, more than this, make a living.

Establishing the relationship of artist and audience is also a useful preliminary to the critical assessment of this poet's work. The obstacles to such an assessment lie in the incongruity of applying the conventional apparatus of academic criticism, which is concerned essentially with questions of meaning and interpretation, to a body of work which is frankly popular in expression and appeal. The methodology of modern criticism is especially adapted to the elucidation of masterpieces and tends to become arbitrary when called on to interpret the work of a minor, popular writer. Even such minor poets as Thomas Gray and William Collins, who may be thought to have produced a few perfect poems, do not appear to lend themselves to the kind of interpretation favored by current critical methods. And, in the case of Riley, there are no masterpieces, no "perfect poems," and only a handful of passably good ones among the general mass of what must be, even to the most unexacting standards, bad work. To assess it in terms of these standards would involve a wholesale rejection.

The analysis of Riley's work must be directed, therefore, primarily towards determining why it appealed so conspicuously to the taste of the age and how Riley was able to shape it to have such great popular appeal. There is, in fact, no "development" in Riley's work after the 1880's (and thus another *raison d'être* of the academic critical method is lacking); but there was, in the 1870's and in the early 1880's, a "trying-out" of various styles and themes until the ideal (and ideally remunerative) combination was arrived at. It is necessary to consider what these styles and themes were, the manner in which Riley inherited them from previous writers, and the mode in which he adapted them for his own purposes.

Though Riley cannot be said to have "influenced" his contemporaries or successors (apart from a number of very minor imitators in his own lifetime), there can be no doubt that the influence of his popular reworkings of certain themes—in particular those of contented small-town life and the comic rustic philosopher—was important in American literary history. It transmitted to the next generation of American writers certain aspects of popular mythology which, on a lower level, are as significant as the "certain habitual story" of "a divinely granted second chance for the human race" in the myth of the American Adam.[15] In fact, it may be possible to see in Riley's reworkings of popular mythology merely the debasement of the more fundamental mythology of Walt Whitman. In this process the "simple separate person" of the "Song of Myself" becomes the solitary, contented, semiliterate rustic of the "Johnson of Boone" poems, or the paradisal, undemanding limitation of "The Little Town o' Tailholt" is a version of the American Eden with which the most everyday intelligence was familiar.

It was the Rileyan version of the small-town myth which Edgar Lee Masters, Sinclair Lewis, Thornton Wilder, and others inherited—and rejected or adapted to their own ends. The historic-critical approach to Riley's work should therefore assist not merely in reconstructing some aspects of the popular taste of the late nineteenth century but also in determining in what manner the thematic material of the popular literature of this period, as well as its assumptions and attitudes, influenced the succeeding generation of American writers.

A final aim is to suggest some possible ways in which the work of a minor poet like Riley can be enjoyed in terms of the taste of the present age. This may be in part a matter of making the effort towards the acquisition of antiquarian taste. In this way, present-day collectors of Victorian furniture and painting have inflated the prices of the art objects of that era while modern art critics have yet to evolve a critical terminology by which these objects may be "appreciated." Though modern literary taste has yet to develop an affinity with the work of the great majority of minor Victorian and nineteenth-century American poets, modern literary criticism faces the same difficulties in evolving an adequate critical terminology and technique in dealing with their work.

The tastes and the anxieties of our own age (which has a taste for anxiety) are reflected in the literary critic's preference for the Satanic, the troubled, the problematic in nineteenth-century literature, in American literature the "alienated." Inevitably, therefore, the more unalienated aspects of the nineteenth-century writer tend to be overlooked. Tennyson's "English Idyls" interest us less than "Maud," Hardy's *Under the Greenwood Tree* less than *Tess of the D'Urbervilles*. The more "popular" styles of other writers are also given scant attention. Though the Satanic aspect of Poe receives its due of analysis, modern criticism can make little of the popular pieces, "The Bells," "Ulalume," and "The Raven." It is increasingly the troubled and the macabre aspects of Dickens which engage the attention of literary critics while the sunnier and more sentimental aspects, which earned him his great audience, now cause little but embarrassment outside the public school classroom. James Whitcomb Riley was the supremely unalienated poet of nineteenth-century America. To consider his work and the universality of its appeal is an exercise in the restoration of historical perspective in the study of American literature of the last century.

CHAPTER *2*

# Backgrounds

THE LIFE of the Hoosier poet has all the ingredients of a
Horatio Alger story with the plot ironically inverted, for the
means of success are themselves a denial of the Alger ideal. Riley
passes from an authentic barefoot boyhood to metropolitan afflu-
ence by means of the great popularity of his poems celebrating
the superiority of rural simplicity.

Some consideration of his early environment is necessary to understand the kind of poetry he wrote and the kind of audience for
which he wrote. Greenfield in 1849 was like the Sauk Centre of
Sinclair Lewis's childhood—"Thirty years before there was nothing here but native earth." [1] Hancock County, in which Greenfield was situated, had been formed in 1827. When Riley's parents
settled there in 1844, Greenfield was fifteen years old, "a village of
300 inhabitants" and a "neighbor to the primeval forest." The
poet's first biographer quotes the report of a Mass Convention of
this date referring to settlers "emerging from the beech woods
around our peaceful village." "Less than two score years before
Reuben Riley [the poet's father] came to Greenfield," Marcus
Dickey notes, "the Delaware Indians were tramping up and down
Brandywine,[2] to and from their hunting grounds, then located in
the wilderness, now known as Shelby and Bartholomew Coun-
ties." [3]

The National Road, the chief route for settlers moving west
from Ohio and the eastern states, reached Greenfield in 1833. It
was not planked until 1852, but the Indiana Central Railroad had
passed through Greenfield on a line roughly parallelling the
National Road in 1851. Greenfield was thus barely emerging from
the pioneer stage of its existence in the 1850's and was situated
squarely on one of the most important routes by which settlers
travelled to the West.

But it would be misleading to think of this community in terms of frontier lawlessness or even the kind of cultural crudity and nullity which Matthew Arnold was later to deplore in *Civilization in the United States,* the "moral, hard, unloving, unlovely, unrelieved, unbeautified, grinding life" Miss Bird found in Colorado.[4] Indeed, all the indications are to the contrary. Richard Crowder, in his *Those Innocent Years* (1957), cites details of the controversy concerning public and private schools in Greenfield in the 1840's and 1850's. The community favored private schools and made continuing efforts to provide one. The Greenfield Academy, opened in 1855, was at least the third attempt to provide such a school.

"The Midwest had not been settled by barbarians," Crowder reminds us, "but by people from cultivated communities. As they moved toward the frontier, they built schoolhouses and courthouses; they brought with them the principles of education and the law." There was even a county library which suffered a checkered existence through the same period, was reported "impoverished" at the end of 1851, and apparently terminated soon after when the librarian bought the remaining book stock and resigned. Some of these volumes later came into Riley's hands.

## I  *The Riley Family*

Riley's own family had some claims to social and cultural distinction. The father, Reuben,[5] a prosperous lawyer in antebellum days, was appointed school examiner in 1850 and again in 1854. He became Greenfield's first mayor in 1852, and was the youngest member of the state legislature when elected in 1844, serving under Governor James Whitcomb, for whom he named his son.

The artistic proclivities of the family are also worth noting. Riley's maternal grandfather, John Marine, who had moved to Indiana from North Carolina in 1825, set up a mill in Randolph County, wrote his autobiography in rhyme, laid out the town of Rockingham, and advertised the lots in rhyme. "The Marines," Marcus Dickey states, "were flat-boat builders, millers, and versemakers." John Marine was also at times a teacher and a preacher. The poet's mother, Elizabeth Marine, contributed poems to the newspapers of Greenfield and Hancock County; and the father, Reuben, who had had a six-month spell as editor of a short-lived county newspaper in 1847, also had published poems in the local papers. The music-making activities of the family are also noted by the biographers.

This type of amateur culture-making is commonplace in communities in the early postpioneer stage and is the very natural and commendable result of the desire for some distinction in lives which had for long been preoccupied entirely with the need to make a living. It is easy to patronize this, as Twain does—somewhat fondly and with considerable fun at Huck's frontier naïveté—in the descriptions of the Grangerfords' home in *Huckleberry Finn*. Matthew Arnold was no doubt right to scorn the claim of "the writer in the *Atlantic Monthly*" that, "in the smaller cities of the interior, in the northern, middle and southwestern states," he should find "an elegant and simple social order . . . a manner of life belonging to the highest civilization" [6] and to recognize that these claims were frequently shallow.

One of Riley's early prose sketches, "The Gilded Roll," [7] depicts the kind of pleasure which these claims to culture might give, without overrating their seriousness: "But jolly as the days were, I think jollier were the long evenings at the farm. After the supper in the grove . . . , after the lounge upon the grass, and the cigars, and the new fish stories, and the general invoice of the old ones, it was delectable to get back to the girls again, and in the old 'best room' hear once more the lilt of the old songs."

After singing and card-playing, "the oldest Mills girl, who thinks cards stupid anyhow," rouses the company of young people to more serious business: "'. . . this game's just ending and I shan't submit to being bored with another. I say "pop-corn" with Billy!' And after that, she continues, rising and addressing the party in general, 'we must have another literary and artistic tournament, and that's been in contemplation and preparation long enough; so you gentlemen can be pulling your wits together for the exercises, while us girls see to the refreshments'."

And the literary tournament follows, with the entries printed in full. They turn out to be three poems of what were to become the three chief Rileyan types—"A Backward Look," a sentimental, nostalgic evocation of a village boyhood (but not in dialect, as most of the later examples were to be); "Billy's Alphabetical Animal Show" (a series of alphabetical limericks, in the vein of Ed-

ward Lear, but with less of his startling grotesquerie); and "Beautiful Hands," a love poem in the best—or worst—style of the
ladies' magazines of the period:

> When first I loved, in the long ago,
> And held your hand as I told you so.

## II  *Culture Seeking*

It would be foolish to overrate the cultural value of this kind of
activity, and Riley himself would have been the last person to do
so. But it persisted as part of the Middle Western way of life, and
it is amusing to find Sinclair Lewis participating in a similar kind
of cultural party with the literary ladies of Carmel in 1909.[8] Some
of the dangers of taking this kind of culture too seriously are set
forth by Lewis in the account of Carol Kennicott's experiences
with the Gopher Prairie Dramatic Association.

Much of this culture-seeking may be attributed to the desire for
social status in a period before status symbols became largely material. Some of it also became a matter of regional pride, part of
the desire to equal the East in artistic achievement, to produce
"our own Western writers" equal to any the East could produce.
We have seen the importance Riley attached to the achievement
of recognition by the Eastern critics in the 1880's. This was an
admission of subservience which became less and less necessary as
the century drew to a close. Twain had achieved full acceptance
in these years for a form of humor which took much of its point
from the "guying" of the genteel tradition. In much of Riley's most
popular work, frontier crudity and barbarity are softened into
rural, settled simplicity and geniality. The West is "genteelized,"
but it loses none of its essential virtues.

The Western Association of Writers was formed in 1886 to pro-
mote the interests of the nascent Western literary movement. By
the 1900's, when Lew Wallace of Crawfordsville, Indiana, and
Riley himself had won large national audiences, the battle was, in
a sense, won, and the Boston papers could comment, half-jok-
ingly, that the national literary capital was now Indianapolis, with
Riley and Booth Tarkington in residence and Lew Wallace not far
distant in Crawfordsville. In fact, though the publishing capital

had become, and was to remain, New York, the dispersal of writing talent had begun and has since persisted.

The beginning of Riley's writing career coincided with the growing interest in literary matters in Indiana. The Minerva Society, said to be the first literary club for women in the United States, had been formed in New Harmony about 1857. In 1877, the Parlor Club, a literary society, was founded in Lafayette. In 1878, the Greenfield Literary Club was formed; and the following year, the Greenfield Reading Club. The young Riley and a brother and sister joined both groups. In 1877 the Indianapolis Literary Club was formed. The club invited Riley to give them a reading a year later. At this time he had published relatively little work of his own, and he included in his readings popular recitation favorites by other writers.

Literary interests and verse-making were clearly a natural and normal thing for a young man in Riley's environment, and they even had a certain social value. To try to make a living from them was, however, something different; and Riley appears to have developed his talent to this end, in the early stages at least, largely by accident. His experiences with patent-medicine shows, ludicrous as they appear, set him in the right direction. They were, at the time, simply a young man's means of having a good time; but, by putting him in the role of an entertainer who had to sell a product, they quickly established for him the need of winning an audience—and the lesson of quick cash returns for a pleasing performance was learned. If we are tempted to see these experiences as the contemporary equivalent of a spell in sponsored radio, it should be remembered that the material Riley was developing for these performances—ballads like "Farmer Whipple—Bachelor" or monologues like "Tradin' Joe"—were, no matter how sentimentalized, based on the life of the Indiana farmer; and they also made some attempt at conveying the natural forms and rhythms of Hoosier speech, as these lines from "Tradin' Joe" may illustrate:

> Marshall Thomas,—a friend o' mine,
> Doin' some in the tradin' line,
> But a'most too *young* to know it all—
> On'y at *picnics* er some *ball!*—
> Says to me in a banterin' way,

As we was a-loadin' stock one day,—
'You're a-huntin' a wife, and I want you to see
My girl's mother, at Kankakee!'

Much of the poet's skill in rendering the natural flow of speech, its asides and "fill-ins," without straining the grammar or padding unduly, is evident here, as is his ability to hit off touches of character in both narrator and subject in a single line (the third quoted) and the true yarner's ability to sustain interest with a dramatic opening that leaves the listener waiting for the next development.

Riley played the guitar also on his selling tours. The commercial jingle of today had its origin in the work of ballad-singing drummers of the nineteenth century, and the combination of poetry and guitar-playing was continued by another Middle Western "poet of the people," Carl Sandburg. Sandburg, however, raises the work of the guitar-playing balladeer to a level of significant social commentary. It would be absurd to make this claim for Riley's early work; he was, then as later, simply exploiting a popular art form for commercial purposes.

### III  Newspaper Experience

Riley's five months with the *Anderson Democrat* drove home the lessons of the patent-medicine wagon in more literate surroundings. He wrote Lee O. Harris in July, 1877, "I think the newspaper school an excellent one and filled with most valuable experience." [9] His main task was to "write up," with humorous embellishments, the prosy reports of local contributors. He found a natural outlet for his talents in writing commercial jingles which depended for their humor on the commonplace things—oddities of names and crudities of merchandise—and which above all could win the reader into buying. He was writing to induce a rural public to buy in the town, and, as Marcus Dickey comments, "The keynote of his success lay in this, the establishment of a friendly relation between town and country—and he was about the first man in America to do it." The importance of this relationship between town and country, which Riley could play off in a reverse direction, is discussed in a later chapter.

The success of such Riley efforts as the "Rhyme-Wagon," a column on small-town sights and incidents that worked in comic "commercials," was such that in four months the circulation of the paper increased from four hundred to twenty-four hundred subscribers. This period was also the first "trying out" one for Riley, something the newspaper made especially easy. Certain prose sketches in a fantastic vein—"The Duck Creek Jabberwock," "Unawanga-wawa," "Trillpipe's Boy on Spiders" [10]—date from this time, which also saw the beginning of Riley's vein of jabberwocky in verse, in such poems as "Craqueodoom" and "A Wrangdillion." Riley was to continue to work this vein for some years; and his "fantastick drama in verse," *The Flying Islands of the Night,* his most ambitious effort in this style, is discussed in the next chapter. "Craqueodoom," the earliest published poem of this type, was an inauspicious beginning:

> The quavering shriek of the Fly-up-the-creek
> Was fitfully wafted afar
> To the Queen of the Wunks as she powdered her cheek
> With the pulverized rays of a star.
>
> . . . . . . . . . . . . . . . .
>
> And the air it grew chill as the Gryxabodill
> Raised his dank, dripping fins to the skies,
> And plead with the Plunk for the use of her bill
> To pick the tears out of his eyes.

Lewis Carroll with a Middle Western accent does not convince, and the imitation is generally unsuccessful because it lacks the obsessive and tantalizing logic of Carroll. Riley continued to work in this style, but it met with little success then or later. The style was a part of the process of "trying out," and it eventually found its appropriate form in the whimsical inventiveness and mock-macabre terrors of some of the children's poems. One of Riley's first children's poems, it may be noted, appeared in the *Anderson Democrat.* [11]

## IV  *The "Leonainie" Hoax*

This first valuable experience of newspaper work terminated abruptly as a result, we may suppose, of Riley's overweening ambition to succeed as a poet. The need for recognition in the East was obsessive even at this date, and it led Riley and some friends to publish in a local paper, the *Kokomo Dispatch*, an alleged newly discovered poem by Poe, "Leonainie," that was, in fact, a slight and not very skillful imitation by Riley. This was the age of the newspaper hoax, and the intention of the hoaxers was usually to prove a point. The intention here was to prove that a new work by an established writer would receive immediate praise and recognition, whereas a similar work by an unknown would not. The thought is not new, but the hoax was relatively successful. When the poem was noted or reprinted in New York, Chicago, Cincinnati, Boston, and other city newspapers, the comment was about equally for and against authenticity. The hoaxers "particularly wanted notices in the *Atlantic* and *Scribner's*." "They are the critics," J. O. Henderson, the editor of the *Kokomo Dispatch*, said.[12] Exposure eventually came less than a month later through two rival Kokomo papers.

Riley later described the hoax as "the outgrowth simply of an idle scheme of mine," [13] but the tone of his original letter to Henderson, allowing for the element of conspiratorial fun, suggests an astute bid to set his name before a larger public:

> If we succeed—and I think sheer audacity and tact sufficient capital to assure that end,—after fooling the folks a little and smiling o'er the encomiums of the press, you understand, we will 'rise up William Riley' and bu'st our literary bladder before a bewildered and enlightened world!!!
>
> I write you this in all earnestness and confidence, trusting you will help me perfect the project—for should I use the 'Democrat' as the medium of its introduction, people would 'drop' most likely, and my bloom of hope be 'nipped in the bud'.—So in my need I come to you, feeling that the benefit, if any may arise— will be mutual.[14]

Whatever the motive, the hoax was unsuccessful; and Riley's ambitions were left to hang fire. That he was drivingly ambitious for success is apparent from the unguarded statements in some of his letters to Elizabeth Kahle. In spite of the geniality and humor, Riley's letters are characteristically guarded; but the tone of a literary Alger hero, with a streak of melancholy disillusionment, comes through unmistakeably:

*Feb. 29, 1880.* I am intensely eager to win something of a name since it seems that all things else must be denied.

*July 6, 1880.* It's almost wrong, I think with you sometimes, to work with the ambition that I do. But I am eager to succeed—so feverish in my desire to be something and somebody—that my effort never flags or falters for a minute; but self-impelled, moves on and on, gathering newer force and power with each succeeding hint of final victory.

*June 23, 1881.* Home may be a dull place, but the world is ten times worse and it does jostle so! and O the thousand and one little mean treacheries one meets! To escape them and ride over them and trample them down-down-down where they belong, one must have the money-scepter in one's fist. Then be a king indeed.[15]

## V   *Reading Tours*

The process of finding acceptable forms to win a large audience was more successful, though not at first very remunerative, in Riley's public readings. Beginning in 1876, his readings in the churches and schoolhouses of small towns in the Middle West, together with his later success as resident rhymester and humorist on the *Indianapolis Journal*, resulted in his being signed for the Redpath Lyceum Bureau circuit in 1881. This contract in turn led to his very successful appearances in the East.

These years were devoted to perfecting his platform technique and to devising various forms for the presentation of his material. "My lecture on Funny Folks is nearly complete," he writes in October, 1876. He had got his cue from the annual forecast of talent for the lecture platform. The bureaus were calling for humorists— Petroleum V. Nasby for "Betsey Jane," Twain for "Buck Fanshaw's Funeral," Josh Billings reading from his "Almanac," Bret Harte on "The Progress of American Humor."[16] For three years in the late 1870's Riley's parody lectures on Robert Ingersoll and "Benson out-Bensoned," satirizing the excesses of the atheist and the temperance fanatic, were tried out and eventually dropped. "No more mocking-bird business," was Riley's comment,[17] and its significance appears in the discussion of his later adaptation of the "cracker barrel philosopher" tradition in the "Johnson of Boone" poems.

In September, 1879, Riley prepared a serious lecture on "Poetry

and Character," which included recitations of such poems as
Longfellow's "The Day Is Done" and his own "Farmer Whipple—
Bachelor" and "An Old Sweetheart of Mine" and which also incor-
porated a defense of dialect in verse. By the time of the first Boston reading, humor and dialect were predominant. About 1884,
the title became "Eccentricities of Western Humor"; later still it
was "Characteristics of the Hoosier Dialect." In 1887, when
Riley's impact as a public personality was assured, the lecture format was discontinued, and "An Evening with Riley" meant simply
the recitation of favorite pieces with comic interludes of introduction and comment.

If the Middle West and its cultural societies were hungry for
culture and would pay to bring Dickens, Arnold, Henry Irving,
Ellen Terry, Sarah Bernhardt, Adelina Patti—the finest literary,
theatrical and musical talent of Europe—for their entertainment
and enlightenment, there was also an element of bourgeois obliga-
tion about its culture-seeking, as Arnold noted in Chicago in
1883.[18] Many audiences preferred to be entertained rather than
enlightened. When Riley and Bill Nye went on tour together,
their "symposium" was advertised as "not a lecture" in order to
annul any suspicions. We may regard this precaution as an example of what Richard Hofstadter calls "the case against intellect" in
the nineteenth century and Riley as one of the "incomplete and
truncated minds" he finds in American letters.[19] It is indeed part of
the "rejection of 'aristocratic and feminine and unworldly culture'," but it is motivated perhaps more by sheer unwillingness to
stretch the imagination too far than by "arrant populism, [and]
mindless obsession with 'practicality'." While Melville in 1860
sought in vain to make a living by lecturing on such topics as the
South Seas and the Statuary of Rome,[20] Riley could afford to poke
fun at the whole lecture business in "The Rossville Lectur'
Course," a dialect piece he would recite while on tour with Bill
Nye, about some small-town folks who "got up a Lectur' Course,"
wrote to the Bureau, found that ". . . blame! ef forty dollars
looked like anything at all," and finally settled for Bill Nye as their
lecturer.

Riley, who had learned his lesson, stated it in this way:

In my readings I had an opportunity to study and find out for
myself what the public wants and afterward I would endeavour

to use the knowledge gained in my writing. . . . The public desires nothing but what is absolutely natural, so perfectly natural as to be fairly artless. It can not tolerate affectation, and it takes little interest in the classical production. It demands simple sentiments that come direct from the heart. . . . I learned to judge and value my verses by their effect upon the public.[21]

Marcus Dickey does not date this statement, and it may be that it was obtained from the author himself when the official biography was in preparation during the last years of the poet's life. It implies that we are to seek in Riley's most popular work simplicity of diction, naturalness of phrasing, an avoidance of "literary" treatment, and that "grasp of the plain emotions of plain people (or stereotyped emotions of stereotyped people)" which Wallace Stegner singles out as Riley's special quality.

Although Riley had hit the right note as early as 1871 in a poem like "What Smith Knew About Farming" and had returned to it again in 1874 in the already mentioned "Farmer Whipple—Bachelor" and "Tradin' Joe," it was to be almost a decade before he brought this style, and his own popularity, to full fruition. In the interval he tried a variety of currently popular styles, and he made considerable effort toward winning fame as a writer of prose sketches. An analysis of these sketches and of Riley's single verse drama is the subject of the next chapter.

## VI  *Publishing History*

The nineteenth century saw the beginning of those mutually profitable and mutually exploitative relationships of writer and publisher that are a commonplace of the publishing business in the twentieth century. There can have been few more successful or more skillfully managed collaborations in the nineteenth century than that of Riley and the Bobbs-Merrill Company, which began in the fall of 1883 when Merrill, Meigs and Company (as it then was) brought out a second edition of *The Old Swimmin' Hole*. The relationship lasted until Riley's death, and has continued in effect until the present day when, although the one-volume trade edition of the *Complete Poetical Works* is now published by Grosset & Dunlap, many items of Rileyana, including Richard Crowder's biography of 1957, continued to appear from the Bobbs-Merrill Company.

Following *The Old Swimmin' Hole,* the prose sketches and poems of *The Boss Girl* appeared in 1885. There followed a series of volumes, all in large part collected from work first published in newspapers and magazines, starting with *Afterwhiles* in 1887 and ending with *Fugitive Pieces* in 1914. Many of the volumes contained little or no new material but were regroupings, differently presented or more attractively illustrated, of familiar material. This total exploitation of the established favorite was, of course, a common device of the popular entertainer until television produced the problem of "overexposure" and the constant hunger for fresh material.

From first to last, there were more than ninety titles by Riley on the Bobbs-Merrill trade list. The "original" volumes, sixteen in all, appeared in two formats: the "Greenfield" edition for the trade constituted the first edition; and the "Homestead" edition, for subscribers, appeared a year or so later in a handsomer binding, sometimes with additional material and more attractive presswork. Two of the sixteen volumes were first published by the Century Company and one by Scribner's, both New York firms; but these volumes were also later taken over by Bobbs-Merrill.

In the Riley Centennial Year, 1949, Bobbs-Merrill tried to estimate how many Riley books had been sold.[22] The figure was well toward the three million mark when it was discovered that the record of sales before 1893 was no longer in existence. Books by Riley were favorite gift items in the three decades from 1880 to 1910, and the Russos' bibliography records that publication dates of many of the volumes were advanced to catch the Christmas gift market. Collections by category, *Riley Farm-Rhymes, Riley Love-Lyrics, Riley Songs o' Cheer,* and others were one form of publication. Immensely popular were the volumes presenting a single "best-loved" poem in decorative, illustrated format, and *An Old Sweetheart of Mine* and *The Orphant Annie Book* are outstanding among these. Of the many illustrated editions, the two series by Howard Chandler Christy and Will Vawter were the most popular and successful, though the illustrations by Ethel Franklin Betts for *Little Orphant Annie* made a popular single volume.

There were five "Christy-Riley" books and seven "Deer Creek" or Vawter-Riley volumes. In effect, the two series constitute the two sides of the image of Riley as a popular poet. The "Christy-Riley" volumes, of which *An Old Sweetheart of Mine* was the crowning success, exemplify the rather lugubriously sentimental "Victorian" poet of tender love experienced in youth, consecrated in marriage, and recalled in old age. There is a distinctly middle-class, comfortably settled air about Christy's figures. The books illustrated by Vawter, who was also, like Riley, born in Greenfield, personify the folksy, Hoosier side of Riley in figures often poorly drafted but constituting a picture gallery of an idealized rural America of the mid-nineteenth century—one full of picket fences, hollyhocks, old-fashioned roses, picturesque old men, handsome swains, barefoot boys, slow plowhorses, and trim, frame houses.

The Biographical edition of the complete works in 1913 was a ponderously impressive publication, issued in five bindings, from green cloth to full morocco; and, two years later, it was made available in soft leather on thin paper. These facts alone should testify to the continuing éclat of Riley's popular reputation to the end of his life. The Biographical edition was in fact reissued as the Memorial edition, in ten volumes, a few months after Riley's death in 1916. The Biographical edition is an excellent piece of editing by Edmund H. Eitel, Riley's nephew and secretary; and, since it was edited with Riley's help, it provides a definitive text. Extensive bibliographical information is given, and well over two hundred poems are here first collected. It is a comment of some kind on the vagaries of literary reputation that the works of Poe and Melville still lack, and those of Whitman and Hawthorne are only now receiving, the editorial attention which the work of James Whitcomb Riley received in his lifetime.

## VII  *Literary Finance*

If Riley was fortunate with his publishers, he was much less so with the managers of his reading tours, at least until his brother-in-law, Henry Eitel, was given the position in 1890 and could act to negotiate favorable terms with the tour managers. Until this time Riley was at the mercy of those who had created him as a platform personality, and there can be no doubt that his popular appeal was ruthlessly exploited and that his health was seriously impaired by the strenuous program of tours which his managers arranged for him. From the 1890's on, a series of periods of debilitating weakness kept him confined at home for months at a time; and, in his last years, a succession of mild strokes preceded his death from heat prostration in August, 1916, an ironic end for one who loved the summer.

The part his reading tours played in establishing his popular success is readily apparent; but, once established, this success brought sizeable profits, often over one thousand dollars a night in the big cities, for his tour managers. When the touring partnership with Bill Nye was begun in 1886, both had considerable national fame; but the notorious Major James B. Pond, of the Redpath Lyceum Bureau, who managed most of Riley's appearances through the 1880's, wrote to Twain (who had introduced the Nye-Riley combination to Boston audiences) in these terms: "I will go partners with you, and I will buy Nye and Riley's time and give an entertainment something like the one we gave in Boston. Let it be announced that you will introduce the 'Twins of Genius.' Ostensibly a pleasure trip for you. I will take one-third of the profits and you two-thirds. I can tell you it will be the biggest thing that can be brought before the American public." [23]

For whatever reasons, Twain did not accept the offer; but Pond, and later the Western Lyceum Agency, needed no help. When Nye and Riley, on different occasions, had to break off their tours because of ill health, the partnership was finally dissolved after the collapse of Riley in drink and despair at Louisville, Kentucky, in January, 1890. His recovery marked in effect the beginning of his financial prosperity and the end of his creative years. With Henry Eitel managing his business affairs, his tours, which were gradually curtailed from this point on, could be arranged conveniently and profitably. They often became part of a roving vacation.

Riley was now in full attainment of his great national popularity, and this was the time when he might have moved elsewhere, to the real centers of literary influence—Boston or New York—if he had chosen. Instead, we find him writing to Madison Cawein in 1891 that "no money could tempt me ever to quit my home and people." [24] In the summer of 1893 he began his abode as a permanent paying guest, the bachelor boarder, at the home of Major Charles L. Holstein on Lockerbie Street; and it remained his home until his death. The same year he bought "The Old Homestead" in which he had passed most of his childhood, in Greenfield, and it became his summer residence. In later years he spent the coldest months in Florida.

The Riley of the latter years was elegantly, fastidiously dressed, with goldheaded cane and boutonnière, the "small, compact, dignified gentleman" who could on the platform become as if by some miracle of gesture and attitude the carelessly dressed, wide-eyed country boy his poems described. While the Lockerbie Street home, with its heavy elegance and solid respectability, suited the citified dignity of the later Riley, the Old Homestead represented his hold on the simple rural values of his Greenfield boyhood. He had attained to urban refinement by celebrating rural simplicity, and he did not neglect his debt to that simplicity.

During the last two decades of Riley's life, it was a frequent pastime of the nation's newspapers to speculate on the reasons for Riley's great popularity. Although some possible sociological explanations for the wholesale identification by the citizenry with Riley's idyls of golden boyhood and rustic simplicity are offered in later chapters of this book, much of Riley's success as a public personality must be attributed to his surpassing skill as a reader of his own work, a fact attested to by many authorities, most notably by Irving and Twain. But more than this, Riley was as a popular versifier all things to all people. He had a remarkably wide range of forms and styles, broadly divided into his "Hoosier" style in dialect verse and his "Lockerbie" style in modern English. His collected poems, before the Biographical edition appeared, were drawn together into two "books" with these descriptive epithets. The two divisions might be further subdivided into love lyrics, sentimental poems of parting and sorrow, patriotic poems, formal obituary tributes, richly characterized narratives of farm and small-town life, nonsense poems, the comic philosophical verses of the "Johnson of Boone" series, and the children's poems, which themselves covered a wide range from sentimental and lyrical to narrative and descriptive. Only in dialect does Riley achieve any strongly marked individuality, but a few of the modern English pieces were among his most popular work.

Since there was no "development" in Riley's verse in the usual critical sense, it would therefore be misleading to follow a chronological pattern in attempting a critical consideration of his work. Instead, I have preferred a consideration grouped according to his various styles. While this approach may appear to place undue emphasis on the most meretricious part of his work, that in modern English, at the expense of his work in dialect, it should be noted that the study of popular verse of this order has little concern with merit, which may be almost totally lacking in any absolute poetic sense. Riley's verse was popular whatever his style of the moment, but there were, of course, many individual poems more popular than others. Any examination of his poetry would be incomplete if it did not involve a consideration of all its aspects, without undue regard for their respective value or interest to readers of the present day.

### CHAPTER 3

# Trying Out: Prose Sketches and Verse Drama

RILEY was to say comparatively late in his career that he "could not write prose," but his work in this medium occupies one of the six volumes—some four hundred pages—of the Biographical edition. What he meant was that he could not write prose which would find a large audience. His second published book, *The Boss Girl, A Christmas Story, and Other Sketches,* ten prose sketches alternating with ten poems, when published in 1885 did not attract the attention of public or critics. Writing to an English publisher who had made inquiries about the book in 1888, Riley remarked: "Here—much as I deplore the fact—few but the writer seem at all taken with that work and in consequence all orders lean decidely to verse—and that too in dialect." [1] The book "was, to begin with, unhappily named." In 1891 the title was changed to *Sketches in Prose and Occasional Verses* but without changing the book's fortunes, since sheets from the 1891 edition were still being used in 1895 when Riley's sales were enormous and increasing. His public had come to expect something else by then.

## I *Antecedents of the Prose Sketches*

The ten sketches in *The Boss Girl* and five more which were collected in *Pipes o' Pan at Zekesbury* (1888) had, with one exception, first appeared between 1878 and 1884 in the *Indianapolis Journal.* They are competent, if derivative, attempts in several then fashionable styles. Their interest is partly a biographical one, since some of them provide the "real life" background for some of the poems,[2] and partly stylistic, as indications of the type of material the aspiring popular writer might then choose. Riley was writing for a local audience on his newspaper, but he did so with an eye to a larger market; and there were at this time many "Western" prose writers who had achieved national fame with as many versions of what life in the West came to. The two main alternatives were to tell the truth or to dress it up, to emphasize the crudity and ugliness or the freedom and adventure; and the usual solution was to effect some compromise between the two. The two schools of realism and romance might be said to center in Indiana and California, and the seminal works for each were, respectively, Edward Eggleston's *The Hoosier Schoolmaster* (1871) and Bret Harte's *The Luck of Roaring Camp* (1868). Each had opened a new field, set a new fashion and a new standard for the "local color" novel or story, and had discovered a public for Western material which neither had imagined to exist, as the well-known quotation from Eggleston's preface to *The Hoosier Schoolmaster* suggests:

> It has been on my mind since I was a Hoosier boy to do something toward describing life in the back country districts of the Western states. It used to be a matter of no little jealousy with us, I remember, that the manners, customs, thoughts and feelings of New England country people filled so large a place in books while our life, not less interesting, not less romantic, and certainly not less filled with humorous and grotesque material, had no place in literature. It was as though we were shut out of good society. And, with the single exception of Alice Cary, perhaps, our Western writers did not dare speak of the West otherwise than as the unreal world to which Cooper's lively imagination had given birth.[3]

The Eggleston note of earthy realism is struck on the first pages of *The Hoosier Schoolmaster* when the young teacher meets "old Jack Means, the school trustee," and is warned that,

> You see, we a'n't none of your saft sort in these diggins. It takes a *man* to boss this deestrick. Howsumdever, ef you think you kin trust your hide in Flat Crick schoolhouse, I ha'n't got no 'bjection. But ef you git licked don't come on us. Flat Crick don't pay no 'nsurance, you bet! Any other trustees? Wal, yes. But as I pay the most taxes, t'others jist let me run the thing. You can begin right off on Monday. They a'n't been no other

applications. You see it takes some grit to apply for this school.
The last master had a black eye for a month.[4]

Though Harte can be equally realistic, for example, in the details of "The Old Man's" life in the cabin in "How Santa Claus
Came to Simpson's Bar" or of Wan Lee's death from stoning by
anti-Chinese rioters in "Wan Lee, the Pagan," the real interest of
his stories is the romantic incident for which this realism provides
a setting, incidents such as Dick's fantastic ride on the mare Jovita
in the first of these stories, Betsy Baker's equally fantastic ride in
"The Postmistress of Laurel Run," or the dramatic exposure of the
source of Islington's mysterious and tarnished wealth (working a
new twist on the plot of *Great Expectations*) in "Mrs. Skagg's
Husbands." Harte leaves little to the imagination, but he frequently overstimulates it; and his stereotyping of character in
such figures as Jack Hamlin, the gambler who doesn't miss a trick
but has his own code of honor, and Yuba Bill, the infinitely loyal
stagecoach driver (a kind of Western Sam Weller), tends constantly to draw his stories away from realism to romance.

There was inevitably much cross-fertilization between the two
vigorous schools of regional literature, and Ima Herron's note on
Eggleston's *The Mystery of Metropolisville* (1873) shows that the
Indiana school, which generally relied on folksy sentiment for its
romance and maintained a flavor of piety in most of what it
wrote, could out-Harte Harte when it wanted to. Miss Herron
notes that, "Though a flood, a double drowning, fights, love affairs
and a penitentiary scene put the stamp of sentiment and melodrama on the plot, Eggleston succeeds, nevertheless, in creating a
boom town such as might have been found by the hundreds during the mid-nineteenth century." [5]

## II  *The Prose Sketches*

One of the earliest of Riley's prose sketches—it is, in fact, a
short story with a somewhat rambling plot—was "An Old Settler's
Story," [6] published in the *Indianapolis Journal* in 1878 and first
collected in *Pipes o' Pan at Zekesbury* ten years later. A good example of that cross-fertilization of the two Western schools already mentioned, its outline recalls that of Eggleston's *Mystery of
Metropolisville*, with fights, a near-drowning, the burning of

miller Ezra's home and mill, a lynching, and some realistic matter on the perils of whiskey: "'Long 'bout the beginnin' o' summer, things had got back to purty much the old way. The boys round was a-gittin' devilish, and o' nights 'specially there was a sight o' meanness a-goin' on."

The setting is an early pioneer Indiana settlement—"The Settlement wasn't nothin' but a baby in them days"—and the uglier details are not spared ("the wettest, rainyest weather; and mud! Law!") nor the general spirit of anarchy ("them days they wasn't no law o' no account"). The narrative is entirely in dialect, which is closer to the Eggleston manner, with none of the "highfalutin'" literary flavor in describing the commonplace which is the source of much of Harte's humor, or that quality of affectionate indulgence for weak humanity which underlies his sentimentality. The narrative of Riley's story, moreover, builds a complete picture of the life of the settlement—the work in the mill; the young men and their fights and periodic backslidings into whiskey-drinking; the prayer-meetings; Daddy Barker's sermons; the Settlement social evening and the songs, stories, and "acting parts"; Wash Lowry, the fiddler and his stock of tunes.

The details of the plot and much of the characterization, however, have all the romance and melodrama of Harte and more. "Bill Bills" (William Williams—the name alone suggests Harte), the romantic antihero, is a tough, scarred mystery-man, perhaps guilty of some crime in the East, whose devoted "wife" eventually turns out to be his sister, whom he keeps with him as a potential hostage if his pursuers should find him, and who herself stays with him in the hope of saving him. Bill's attempts to reform and his backsliding sustain the plot until the melodramatic dénouement when his pursuers appear on the scene. He takes the sister's child with him as hostage, tries to cross the river in darkness and mist, is caught through delaying to save the child, and is swiftly strung up, while the sister is reunited with her husband.

The story is a promising piece of work, and Riley was later to include it, presumably for the faithfulness of its description of settlement life, in his volume *Neghborly Poems* (1891) in which the "Johnson of Boone" poems were available, after the first printing in 1883, until the Biographical edition of 1913. This volume, as a later chapter demonstrates, contains the essential Riley; and the story provides a useful gloss on the poems.

None of the other stories or sketches attempts so elaborate a plot, and none is in dialect. As so often with Riley, when he is not using dialect, he is frequently mannered and strained; and the style creaks. But the variety of treatment, theme, and source is worth noting. Some of the sketches have a rural or small-town setting. "Tod" and "The Boy from Zeeny" [7] are the kind of evocation of a small-town boyhood which was to become all too familiar in many later poems. Tod is the type of prank-playing boy, "a failure in arithmetic," who turns out good in the end, while "The Boy from Zeeny" is a plucky outcast, always breaking limbs but bearing his afflictions with aplomb, always ready for the next prank but with his heart in the right place—the type of boy hero for which *Peck's Bad Boy*,[8] indestructible and infinitely malicious, provides the antitype.

"A Nest Egg" [9] creates the idyllic picture of farm life and rural hearts of gold which Riley was to make the theme of many later poems. The "nest egg" of the sketch is Marthy, the lovely, educated daughter of a kind farmer who says that "she was goin' to be the nest egg of our family, and 'slong as I lived I wanted her at home with me." Marthy loves a lieutenant but loses him to her sister, accepts her lot, and tends the now widowed old man. All in all, she cheerfully accepts a life of fulfillment through sacrifice. The sketch ends, like many of the poems of this type, with a symbolic meal: "I am always thinking that I never tasted coffee till that day; I am always thinking of the crisp and steaming rolls, ored over with the molten gold that hinted of the cloverfields, and the bees that had not yet permitted the honey of the bloom and the white blood of the stalk to be divorced." The self-sacrificing richness of Marthy's character is allied with nature's plenitude without any hint of moralizing, with that insistence on the sunny side, and with that refusal to allow a sour note to intrude which were to become the characteristic Riley manner.

Another sketch, "At Zekesbury," [10] presents a comically unflattering picture of an Indiana small town and county seat in The Grand Old Hoosier State, "as it was used to be howlingly referred to by the forensic stump orator from the old stand in the courthouse yard—a political campaign being the wildest delight Zekesbury might ever hope to call its own." The annual circus was the only local attraction; that, and the rainy season that swelled the "Crick," when "crowds of curious townsfolk struggled down to look upon the watery wonder and lean awe-struck above it, and spit in it, and turn mutely home again."

The point of view here is that of a young man about town (such as it is), and the plot concerns the efforts of two young men to fool a phrenologist who has come to lecture on his subject at the town hall. The two are characterized as types of realist and idealist; and, in a supposed trance, each recites a poem—one a Rileyan dialect piece, and the other an "ideal" poem of "stars above/And lips of love." The joke is that one man is the author of both poems; and the point, if any, is to parade Riley's skill in both genres. This sketch does not follow up a promising beginning, and its only interest is to illustrate Riley's concept of himself as a "realistic" poet in dialect and an "idealistic" poet in "literary" English.

Some of the other sketches are, unexpectedly in Riley, set in the city. The city is Indianapolis, sometimes named as such and with references to actual streets; but the milieu is vaguely realized. In one story, "Jamesy," [11] the real setting is a second-hand version of Dickensian London, while the treatment is that of the Dickensian sentimentalized tragedy of child life. It is, not surprisingly, a Christmas story. Jamesy, a shoe-black, supports a drunken, widowed father and an ailing sister who is "The Boss Girl," the one who sustains what family life is left. "I can imagine that boy's home," one of Jamesy's customers says. "There are dozens like it in the city here—a cellar or a shed—a box car or a loft in some old shop, with a father to chase him from it in his sober interludes, and to hold him from it in unconscious shame when hopelessly drunk."

The narrator does all he can to help the boy until eventually, on Christmas Eve, he prevails on him to take him to the boy's home with gifts for the sister: "Our way veered but a little from the very centre of the city, but led mainly along through narrow streets and alley-ways, where the rear ends of massive business blocks had dwindled down to insignificant proportions to leer grimly at us as we passed little grated windows and low, scowling doors."

In Jamesy's home, the narrator finds "a squabby, red-faced woman sitting on the edge of a low bed," who "leered upon me, but with no salutation"; "upon the floor lay the wretched figure of a man, evidently in the deepest stage of drunkenness"; and in the bed lies the sister. "The little haggard face I bent above was beautiful." At the story's end, the girl refuses the gift of money—"you

must take this money back—you must take it back, for I don't
need it. You must take it back and give it—give it to the poor"—
and, as the reader may have anticipated, she dies.

Riley later stated that he did not like this story.[12] We are not
told his reasons, beyond the misleading nature of its first title. The
handling of the Dickensian setting and sentiment is not without
skill, and the temperance overtones would be sure of popular as-
sent. But the sting in the tail concerning the unequal distribution
of wealth and the neglect of the helpless and needy were not what
the popular audience looked for in a favorite poet and storyteller
in the Gilded Age. Riley did not again attempt the note of social
criticism, even in this muted form; and his rural characters are pre-
eminently poor but happy.

Certain other sketches with a more or less urban setting may be
briefly noted. "The Tale of a Spider," [13] a horror story in the manner of Poe, concerns the obsessional relationship of a writer, given
to solitary work at his desk, and a spider, which gradually ac-
quires mesmeric power over him. It dictates to him by guiding his
pen; and, after each visitation, it touches and presses his hand
with "a keen, exquisite sting." The spider, it appears, is possessed
by love, and finally kills itself by drowning in the writer's inkwell.
Appropriately, the question whether the entire affair is a halluci-
nation induced by the writer's solitary habits is left unanswered.
As an exercise in the comic horrific, the piece is competently done,
for the details of the spider's fantastic motions and the growing
sense of its menace are skillfully enough managed. But there is
not enough individuality to lift the story above that of the average
selection in a typical Christmas supplement of the period.

"A Remarkable Man" [14] is a sketch of a trickster, with some hints
of a Bret Harte treatment in the trickster's redeeming traits; but
the difference is that this one cons a living by means of skillful and
allegedly inspired imitations of Shakespeare, Cervantes, and the
like. The sketch is another attempt to display Riley's virtuosity in
a variety of styles, but the imitations are not very skillful. "The
Eccentric Mr. Clark," another departure, is a harrowing piece of
social realism. The tale concerns whiskey and drug addiction. A
son makes a living in the wholesale liquor business after his father, brother, and finally his mother are dying from alcoholism;
and he himself is able to endure the strain of these familial disas-
ters only by periodic doses of morphine; an accidental overdose

finally causes his death. Death and despair are the end of this story, just as they are of the first three of the *Sketches in Prose.* These endings are quite different from the departure into healing eternity, the "distant, peaceful, shining sea," [15] which ends so many of Harte's stories.

The prose sketches, abortive as they are, for the most part show Riley experimenting amateurishly with various forms of social and psychological realism. To him the dialect poetry which was soon to bring him wide fame was itself a form of realism; it employed the real language of man. But, like the young man in the sketch "At Zekesbury," Riley believed that there was an idealistic side to his talent; and his efforts to develop it led him in an unexpected direction.


### III  *Verse Drama*

*The Flying Islands of the Night* (1891) is on all counts a curious and unlooked-for production for a Middle Western poet of the late nineteenth century, and it apparently bewildered the poet's public as much as the poet himself. When sending a copy of the published book to Charles Warren Stoddard, Riley wrote: "Today mailed you my last book. . . . Tell me quick what's the matter with it and what, in God's name, have I done!" [16] Riley may have felt that this disarming remark would forestall criticism on Stoddard's part. Certainly, the work had received little but adverse criticism to that date; and it has since been almost entirely overlooked. Riley's latest biographer, Richard Crowder, does no more than mention it, and he ignores the controversy following its initial publication.

The three-act play was described by the Bowen-Merrill Company in its advertising copy as "a weird and grotesque drama in verse," and the reviews quoted, presumably the more favorable ones, indicate the contemporary reaction. The *Philadelphia Item* considered that "The verse, while being neither heroic nor lyric, partakes of the character of both. The entire poem is of the nature of a burlesque epic." The *Baltimore News* remarked that "In this book Mr. Riley's peculiar genius displays a force and continuity not intimated in any previous work. The argument and plot are radically different from any known drama, fantastical in the highest degree, and beyond question, his most remarkably quaint and peculiar work, since in it he displays a spirit of ingenuity together with a depth and height of imagination that his work has never hitherto suggested." [17]

Perhaps the simplest method of conveying the flavor of the drama is to quote the list of dramatis personae and the stage directions for the first scene.

## DRAMATIS PERSONAE

| | |
|---|---|
| KRUNG, | King—of the Spirks |
| CRESTILLOMEEM, | The Queen—Second Consort to Krung |
| SPRAIVOLL, | The Tune-Fool |
| AMPHINE, | Prince—Son of Krung |
| DWAINIE, | A Princess—of the Wunks |
| JUCKLET, | A Dwarf—of the Spirks |
| CREECH and GRITCHFANG | Nightmares |

## ACT I

### SCENE—THE FLYING ISLANDS

*Scene I.* Spirkland. Time, Moondawn. Interior of Court of KRUNG. A vast, pendant star burns dimly in the dome above the throne. CRESTILLOMEEM discovered languidly reclining at foot of empty throne, an overturned goblet lying near, as though just drained. The Queen in seeming dazed, ecstatic state, raptly gazing upward and listening. Swarming forms and faces, in air above, seen eerily coming and going, blending and intermingling in domed ceiling-spaces of the court. Weird music. Mystic, luminous, beautiful faces detached from swarm, float, singly, forward, tremulously, and in succession, posing in mid-air and chanting.

The Flying Islands are a Maeterlinckian fairyland in which the forces of evil, represented by Crestillomeem, are in conflict with the forces of good, represented by Krung. Crestillomeem is a resourceful and powerful sorceress of uncertain age, preserving her beauty by magic arts, who is aided in her schemes by Jucklet, the misshapen dwarf she has borne by "a former lord." Krung, an old and tired king, is anxious to retain his power for his son Amphine, who is about to marry Princess Dwainie. The mythic analogues of this fairy-story setting would not be far to seek.

The most successful part of the drama is the fantasy setting, which Riley elaborates and sustains with some skill. A fairyland must have its own ways of measuring time and distance: Crestillomeem speaks of the time "ere we had/Been wedded yet a haed," and Jucklet talks of the distance "round about the palace here/For half a node." *The Flying Islands* has its own gemmology, and Crestillomeem draws Spraivoll into taking part in her machinations by a promise that ". . . thou shalt sing at court, in silken tire,/Thy brow bound with wild diamonds, and thy hair/Sown with such gems as laugh hysteric lights/From glittering quespar, guenk and plennocynth."

The setting for Act II is "A garden of Krung's Palace, screened from the moon with netted glenk-vines and blooming zhoomer-boughs, all glimmeringly lighted with star-flakes." The play is, needless to add, a closet-drama, though it could be produced, with small modifications and with some elaborate lighting equipment. The entire action of the drama takes place by moonlight, and the sense of enchantment, of a land in which earthbound limits and values have no part, is sustained in such passages as that in which Crestillomeem describes the sorceries by which she had caused Krung's daughter to stray and fall off the edge of the flying island on to

> . . . an under-island, then
> Just slow unmooring from our own and poised
> For unknown voyagings of flight afar
> And all remote of latitudes of ours.

Riley's imitations of Lewis Carroll in such early poems as "Craqueodoom" and "The Wrangdillion" had already produced the germ of the idea of the fantasy world of the Spirks and the Wunks. In this drama the fantasy is developed and sustained with something of the startling inventiveness and underlying coherence which are responsible for Carroll's unfailing appeal to the imagination. Dwainie's speech on the scientific endeavors of the sons of Wunkland is one of the most striking examples:

> 'Twas Wunkland's son that alchemized the dews,
> And bred all colored grasses that he wist—

> Divorced the airs and mists and caught the trick
> Of azure-tinting earth as well as sky:
> 'Twas Wunkland's son that bent the rainbow straight
> And walked it like a street, and so returned
> To tell us it was made of hammered shine,
> Inlaid with strips of selvedge from the sun,
> And burnished with the rust of rotten stars:
> 'Twas Wunkland's son that comprehended first
> All grosser things, and took our worlds apart
> And oiled their works with theories that clicked
> In glib articulation with the pulse
> And palpitation of the systemed facts—
> For now our goolores say, below these isles
> A million, million miles, are *other* worlds—
> Not like to ours, but *round,* as bubbles are,
> And, like them, ever reeling on through space,
> And anchorless through all eternity.

This glimpse of the real universe through the perspective of unreality conveys that momentary shock, the sense of the unreality of reality, which is the source of the special appeal of the literature of fairyland to children and of the hold of its best works on the adult imagination.

The first version of *The Flying Islands* dates from the mid-1870's. There are, inevitably, defects in a work written very early in its author's career and without any specific model in form or style.[18] The dialogue, in pseudo-Shakespearian blank verse, combined with the fairy modus operandi and the occasional Middle Western rusticities of phrase, can make an odd mixture at times:

> Spang sprit! my gracious Queen! but thou hast scorched
> My left ear to a cinder! and my head
> Rings like a ding-dong on the coast of death!
> For, patient hate! thy hasty signal burst
> Full in my face as hitherward I came!
> But though my lug be fried to crisp, and my
> Singed wig stinks like a little sun-stewed Wunk,
> I stretch my fragrant presence at thy feet
> And kiss thy sandal with a blistered lip.

Jucklet is, however, a Puck-figure, and the rusticities are appropriate.

The dialogue is varied in other ways. The love scene between Amphine and Dwainie has Amphine improvising in eight-syllable couplets that are a blend of the Tennysonian love poem and the liquid flow and dreamlike langour of certain poems of Poe: [19]

> Ah, help me! but her face and brow
> Are lovelier than lilies are
> Beneath the light of moon and star
> That smile as they are smiling now—
> White lilies in a pallid swoon
> Of sweetest white beneath the moon—
> White lilies in a flood of bright
> Pure lucidness of liquid light
> Cascading down some plenilune,
> When all the azure overhead
> Blooms like a dazzling daisy-bed.—
> So luminous her face and brow,
> The luster of their glory, shed
> In memory, even, blinds me now.

Spraivoll, the Tune-Fool (eventually revealed to be the king's lost daughter who was held under enchantment by Crestillo-meem), speaks an elaborate diction in rhymed couplets and is given to sudden outbursts of song in the nonsense style of "Craqueodoom." Her form of enchanted nonsense and Jucklet's mischievous funmaking complement each other and are familiar qualities in fairy stories.[20] They are appropriately deployed in this drama, Jucklet being punished by Dwainie for his mischief and, in his remorse, beginning the overthrow of Crestillomeem, while Spraivoll becomes a part of the inevitable scene of recognition and reunion at the conclusion.

The chief defect of the drama, and a common one in fairy stories, is the elaboration of the plot without any real motivation. Envy and jealousy prompt the schemings of the wicked, and love moves the actions of the good—timeless motives; but Riley involves them in a complicated plot of deceptions and in obscure family relationships which frequently require explaining at length in static scenes of dialogue before the action reveals them.

In the fairy tale, motivation usually takes some elemental form such as the desire for love, the wish for reunion, or the will to do evil; and the plot may be elaborated from a few simple strands of motive. These defects, inherent in the form, may hardly be counted against the merit of *The Flying Islands of the Night*. What counts in the fairy story is the originality, the ability to startle, of the basic idea and the ingenuity with which the story is evolved. In the latter respect, Riley has few surprises; but the basic idea of the play and the fairy world of its setting are remarkably original in a work of its time and place. They owe nothing to the fairyland existing within a hard and real world of Kingsley's *The Water Babies,* which had appeared in 1863. The moon-drenched court of King Krung is more akin to the enchanted gardens of Maeterlinck's *The Blue Bird* or to Colette's libretto for Ravel's opera *L'Enfant et les Sortilèges;* but the respective dates of these are 1909 and 1916. The basic idea of *The Flying Islands* seems to owe something to the Third Part of Swift's *Gulliver's Travels* (the invented terminology also suggests this), but the parallel cannot be taken far. There are hints of *A Midsummer Night's Dream* in some of the scenes with Jucklet and of *The Tempest* in the parallel of Amphine and Dwainie with Ferdinand and Miranda, but there is no Prospero-figure here, and Dwainie works her own magic. Unless some obscure archetype remains to be discovered, it would appear that *The Flying Islands of the Night* is a strikingly original conception in a fashion which did not become fashionable until thirty or forty years later.

The failure of the play to find an audience was a continuing disappointment to Riley. The earliest version of the work had appeared in the Indianapolis *Saturday Herald* in 1878. It was one of the pieces the aspiring poet sent to Longfellow in September of that year with a request for an appraisal.[21] Longfellow replied encouragingly in general terms, declaring that he had set aside the play for later perusal at leisure, but he did not write again. The work was not ignored by the general public, however, as the Russos note in the standard bibliography of Riley's works: "When it first appeared in the *Saturday Herald* (*Indianapolis*), August 24, 1878, . . . it evoked an editorial of praise from the *Indianapolis News,* but an ironical note by Enos B. Reed in the *People* (*Indianapolis*), which brought about a so-called 'War of Poets'. This 'war' went on for months, with Riley's admirers rallying to his defence in the *Saturday Herald,* and Reed leading a vituperative attack in the *People*."[22] This note concerning two rival and circulation-hungry Middle Western newspapers is indicative of the contemporary status of poetry with the general reading public in America, as well as of the reception of *The Flying Islands.*

There was a rumor during Riley's visit to England in 1891 that he had written "an operatic libretto" which he hoped Sir Arthur Sullivan might set to music.[23] Riley issued a statement (published in *The Critic* of September 26, 1891), denying the rumor with the explanation that "What may have given rise to this report is my taking with me a poetic drama which, for a long time, I have been elaborating. . . . This performance . . . will, as originally intended, first appear as a literary venture—a book—a drama in verse."

*The Flying Islands of the Night* did appear a few weeks later; but, despite the author's endeavors to gain favorable notices from a number of well-known reviewers, it attracted little attention. In a letter to William Dean Howells of January 19, 1892, replying to a request from Howells for poems for *The Cosmopolitan,* Riley begs for an opinion of *The Flying Islands*—"Some time can't you glance the proposition through and tell me?"[24] On October 27, 1896, he wrote to Thomas Bailey Aldrich thanking him for his praise of *The Flying Islands of the Night*: "But (Alas me!) yours is almost the only voice of praise breaking the dense hush that seemed to close over that book at its very birth."[25]

Part of the failure of the book to win an audience may be attributed to its combining a setting and a plot appropriate to a work for children, with a style of diction that only an adult audience of some sophistication would appreciate. The verse drama, though far more promising and accomplished than the prose sketches, was evidently another false step. Riley's later and very popular work for children is conspicuously "unliterary" in style; and his efforts to write for an adult audience in a "literary" manner, avoiding dialect and adopting the style of the popular love lyrics and sonnets of the period, were subsequently to take an entirely different form.

### CHAPTER 4

# The Victorian Poet

IN REPLYING to a request from W. D. Howells for contributions to *The Cosmopolitan*, Riley asked: "But do you want dialect—or serious work—or both." [1] The implication that work in dialect could not be serious is more typical of the general critical attitude of the late nineteenth century than of Riley's attitude to his own work (though perhaps one reason for his general tendency to deprecate its value). Serious poetry was that written in "correct" English, but there was plenty of scope within this style for a greater or lesser admixture of poetic diction for the advocates of simple and natural language, and for those who favored a more ornate style and the use of "classical" (that is, European) models.

As we have seen, Riley favored a plain style. The volume of his collected letters contains several to aspiring poets, in response to the kind of requests for advice which he had occasionally sent to established writers when himself a beginner. A letter to Mrs. R. E. Jones dated August 4, 1880, sets out very clearly Riley's views on this subject:

> Another thing I speak of before leaving this modus-operandi outline of how I write for market—and that is: We are writing for today, and for the general reader—who, by the bye, is anything but a profound or classical scholar. Therefore, it has been, and is, my effort to avoid all phrases, words or reference of the old-time order of literature; and to avoid, too, the very acquaintance of it—because we are apt to absorb more or less of the peculiar ideas, methods, etc. of those authors we read; and as everything is right in its place—so the old authors are right in the past—while new ones must be here in the present. . . . Whenever I am forced to say a commonplace thing it is my effort, at least, to say it as it never has been said before—if such a thing can be done without an apparent strain. [2]

Writing to the same person on December 22, 1880, Riley advises:

"You must, in writing for our modern market, avoid most vigilantly all methods and mannerisms of the old writers in old words, phrases, etc.—for instance, such words as *er'st, wa'st, Thou'rt*—and the numberless others of that order. . . . they can't be used without betraying affectation, strain, superfluity." [3]

## I  *Sources*

These letters were written comparatively early in Riley's career, but at a date when his newspaper reputation was consolidated and he was beginning to gain acceptance by the magazines. There is no reason to doubt the sincerity of Riley's advice, but, in writing "for market. . . . for today—for the general reader," he inevitably wrote (when not writing in dialect) in the currently popular style, which was one deriving—or degenerating—from the poets of early and mid-nineteenth-century England. Lowell, who has the last word on this subject in *A Fable for Critics,* says:

> But what's that? a mass meeting? No, there come in lots
> The American Bulwers, Disraelis and Scotts,
> And in short the American everything-elses
>
> . . . . . . . . . . . . . . . . . .
> With you every year a whole crop is begotten,
> They're as much of a staple as corn is, or cotton;
> Why, there's scarcely a huddle of log-huts and shanties
> That has not brought forth its own Miltons and Dantes;
> I myself know ten Byrons, one Coleridge, three Shelleys,
>
> . . . . . . . . . . . . . . . . . .
> A whole flock of Lambs, any number of Tennysons.[4]

Poe's essay "Mr. Griswold and the Poets" makes the same point. Even if the models were American, the sources of subject-matter and style were still likely to be European. Thus, Riley could advise his friend Elizabeth Kahle that "I'm going to positively forbid your reading that misanthropic old Byron, whose dark foreboding cheerless mutterings you sometimes quote to me; and instead *command* you to read my dear, rare, loveable Longfellow—who, however sad he gets, can always see a glorious promise somewhere on beyond." [5]

Longfellow has the special merit of being both fundamentally optimistic and not belonging to the "old-time order of literature," but Longfellow's work, as Newton Arvin reminds us, was saturated in the literature and culture of Western Europe.[6] In dealing with native subjects, the popular writer of the Gilded Age, no less than one of the pre-Civil War period, was likely to adopt an "English" or "Victorian" style, even if it were obtained secondhand. Of the 159 obscure poetasters (of whom W. D. Howells is one) in the 688 closely printed pages in William T. Coggeshall's anthology *The Poets and Poetry of the West*,[7] not one offers a single contribution in dialect. A few random samples suggest the typical treatment of American subjects: from Moses Brooks' "An Apostrophe to a Mound"—

> Here stood a mound erected by a race
> Unknown in history or poet's song,
> Swept from the earth, nor even left a trace
> Where the broad ruin rolled its tide along.
> No hidden chronicle these piles among,
> Or hieroglyphic monument survives
> To tell their being's date or whence they sprung—
> Whether from Gothic Europe's 'northern hives',
> Or that devoted land where the dread siroc drives—

from Charles A. Jones' "Tecumseh"—

> Where rolls the dark and turbid Thames
> His consecrated wave along,
> Sleeps one, than whose, few are the names
> More worthy of the lyre and song;
> Yet o'er whose spot of lone repose
> No pilgrim eyes are seen to weep;
> And no memorial marble throws
> Its shadow where his ashes sleep—

or from Thomas Gregg's "Song of the Whippowil"—

> The sun hath sunk beneath the west,
> And dark the shadows fall;
> I'll seek again my forest home,
> And make my evening call.
> The zephyr in the grove is hushed,
> And every leaf is still;
> So I will seek my wild retreat,

And chant my Whippowil.
Whippowil! [8]

Derivative poetasting of this kind may be taken as typical of the inheritance of popular culture which the readers and writers of Middle Western newspaper verse would have possessed in the Gilded Age. Robert P. Roberts has emphasized the continuity of popular culture at this period: "The Gilded Age was to a great degree, particularly in the popular arts, a product of the techniques and tastes of pre-Civil War America." [9] Roberts remarks that a "phase of [American] culture rarely dealt with, especially in this period, is the extent to which the traditional classical culture of western Europe belonged to the people and flourished on a popular level," while he notes "the extent to which the traditional cultures of the Western world, albeit sometimes in debased forms, continued to hold sway in America." The great popularity of the derivative culture of English novels and poems in the America of the second half of the nineteenth century is indicated as much by the large number of reprints in America as by the general tendency of popular American writers to imitate these models.

But, if the work of James Whitcomb Riley is any indication, there was a general shift in taste in the Gilded Age. Riley would have rejected the pseudo-Byronic ponderosity of the first two examples quoted from Coggeshall's anthology and the Moore-like tinkle of the third. About half of Riley's total output of verse is in what may be called "literary" (nondialect) English. The greater part of this half consists of poems of "Love," of "Bereavement," of "Art, Poetry and Music," [10] either in a style of lush exoticism compounded of the Tennyson of "Now sleeps the crimson petal," the Elizabeth Barrett Browning of the "Sonnets from the Portuguese," the D. G. Rossetti of the sonnets from "The House of Life," and the "Sonnets for Pictures"—or in the style of jingling, even doggerel, simplicity perpetrated ad nauseam by the school of Eliza Cook and Mrs. Felicia Hemans.

## II   The Love Poems

The Tennysonian exoticism of the love poems frequently merges in Riley's work with a native strain derived from Poe. Two of the poems collected in *Afterwhiles* may be taken to illustrate this. "Illileo" sets the beloved in a Tennysonian moonlit garden but her name is Italianate. She is like Psyche, and her poem has the liquid consonantal flow of Poe:—

> Illileo Legardi, in the garden there alone,
> With your figure carved of fervor, as the Psyche carved of stone,
> There came to me no murmur of the fountain's undertone
> So mystically, musically mellow as your own.

As the consonants fade to a hush (with much alliterative play to flatter the reciter's art), the poem is suddenly charged with an image of suppressed eroticism such as Tennyson might have used—

> . . . the echoes faltered breathless in your voice's vain pursuit;
> And there died the distant dalliance of the serenader's lute:
> And I held you in my bosom as the husk may hold the fruit.

In the concluding lines, the two effects are combined in a note of passion sick to excess—

> A moan goes with the music that may vex the high repose
> Of a heart that fades and crumbles as the crimson of a rose.

The poem is, of course, not a conscious reworking of two styles of love poetry, one native and the other foreign, but a conscious contriving of effects by manipulating the resources of the general mass of love poetry, both English and American, of the mid-nineteenth century. It is not likely that the readers of ladies' magazines would have made the distinction.

Riley's love poetry in general inclines toward the style of Rossetti and his school, often with the associations of antiquity favored by the Pre-Raphaelite poets. This inclination is particularly noticeable in Riley's love sonnets, for example in "Her Hair," which begins:

> The beauty of her hair bewilders me—
> Pouring adown the brow, its cloven tide
> Swirling about the ears on either side
> And storming down the neck tumultuously:

> Or like the lights of old antiquity
>> Through mullioned windows, in cathedrals wide,
>> Spilled moltenly o'er figures deified
> In chastest marble, nude of drapery.

Not infrequently a sepulchral note is added to enrich the passionate mood with a sense of earthly passion enduring beyond the grave, as in the third of the three sonnets entitled "Has She Forgotten," when the lover left alone by the death of the beloved expresses his desire to "Lift from the grave her quiet lips, and stun/My senses with her kisses."

Still another source of European exoticism in the popular love poetry of the Gilded Age was the lyrics and tales of Eastern passion typified by Byron's "Hebrew Melodies" and "Turkish Tales" and by Moore's "Lalla Rookh." This strain was acclimated in the American tradition by such writers as William Wetmore Story, Bayard Taylor, and Thomas Bailey Aldrich, all writers of the generation immediately preceding Riley's who produced their mature work in the 1850's and 1860's. Alfred Kreymborg interprets their choice of material as a means of handling the rawness of the American setting, simply by turning their backs on it.[11] In Story's hands, the style becomes almost an athletic school of love poetry: for example in his "Cleopatra," which describes the meditations of the forsaken queen:

> I will lie and dream of the past time,
>> Aeons of thought away . . .
> When, a smooth and velvety tiger
>> . . . fierce in a tyrannous freedom,
> I knew but the law of my moods . . .
> Till I heard my wild mate roaring,
> As the shadows of night came on . . .
> Then I roused and roared in answer . . .
> And wandered my mate to greet.
> We toyed in the amber moonlight,
>> Upon the warm flat sand,
> And struck at each other our massive arms—
>> How powerful he was and grand!
> Then like a storm he seized me,
>> With a wild triumphant cry,
> And we met, as two clouds in heaven
>> When the thunders before them fly.[12]

Though Riley was clearly anxious to set the pulses of his lady readers a-flutter in his love verses, there is very little material in this style in his work and none in the volume of *Riley Love Lyrics,* in which his verses of this type were collected in 1899. The style was evidently a fashion which was passing, but Riley could work it with the best, as may be illustrated with a quotation from his "The Bedouin":

> O love is like an untamed steed!—
> So hot of heart and wild of speed,
>
> . . . . . . . . . . . . .
> . . . Ah, that my hands
> Were more than human in their strength,
> That my deft lariat at length
> Might safely noose this splendid thing
>
> . . . . . . . . . . . . .
> To grapple tufts of tossing mane—
> To spurn it to its feet again,
> And then, sans saddle, rein or bit,
> To lash the mad life out of it!

The taste of the Gilded Age preferred a more familial type of passion, with only a mild titillation of the wandering fancy, a fact attested by the immense popularity, in books and as a recitation piece, of Riley's "An Old Sweetheart of Mine." No better example could be found of the popular poem of this period. It unites the themes of love, family security, the joys of childhood, and the power of contented middle-class respectability in eighteen four-line stanzas[13] of quietly meditative semidoggerel. The metre is of the type preferred by Eliza Cook and other lady poets of Victorian England, and it would offer no surprises to an American audience.

The situation is that of a settled, mature family man who sits meditating in his study—

> As one who cons at evening, o'er an album, all alone,
> And muses on the faces of the friends that he has known,
> So I turn the leaves of Fancy, till, in shadowy design,
> I find the smiling features of an old sweetheart of mine.

The dreamer is, it vaguely transpires, a poet (awakening sug-gestions of the appeal of the "artistic" life for the popular audience) and thus the more inclined perhaps to give his "truant fancies" rein—

> Though I hear beneath my study, like a fluttering of wings,
> The voices of my children and the mother as she sings—
> I feel no twinge of conscience to deny me any theme
> When Care has cast her anchor in the harbor of a dream.

The sweetheart was a childhood one and recollections of "child-hood-days enchanted" follow, of "The old school bell," the exchange of gifts and kisses, and the future planned "When we should live together in a cozy little cot/Hid in a nest of roses, with a fairy garden-spot."

If there is any hint of unquiet in this quiet enumeration of the standard pleasures of a normal and happy life depicted in clichés which were part of the standard language of the sentimental balladry and song of the time, it lies in the suggestion that the dreamer only dreams these things as a possibility other than the direction his real life has taken. Doubt is removed in the gentle twist of the last stanza—

> But ah! my dream is broken by a step upon the stair,
> And the door is softly opened, and—my wife is standing there:
> Yet with eagerness and rapture all my visions I resign,—
> To greet the *living* presence of that old sweetheart of mine.

The cliché is rounded out, and the dream of love becomes reality in a picture of domestic contentment that justifies the truant fancies, innocent though these were.

"An Old Sweetheart of Mine" is a variation in verse on the typical themes of the sentimental-moralistic novels that were a staple of the weekly story papers and of publishers' lists throughout the second half of the nineteenth century; and the hint of "realism" in the suggestion of marital discontent is itself the cause of the "charm" of the conclusion: the husband's gentle deception becomes a gentle deception of the reader.

### III   *Poetry of Consolation*

Riley was not above mere pastiche in his adaptation of popular Victorian English styles for the North American reader. "The Old

Trundle Bed" is in diction, metre, and tone simply a *rechauffé*—
and a slight improvement—on Eliza Cook's "The Old Arm Chair."
The opening stanzas of the two poems read:

> (*Mrs. Cook*)
> I love it—I love it, and who shall dare
> To chide me for loving that old arm-chair!
> I've treasured it long as a sainted prize—
> I've bedewed it with tears, I've embalmed it with sighs,
> 'Tis bound by a thousand bands to my heart,
> Not a tie will break, not a link will start;
> Would you learn the spell?—A mother sat there,
> And a sacred thing is that old arm-chair.[14]

> (*J. W. Riley*)
> O the old trundle-bed, where I slept when a boy!
> What canopied king might not covet the joy?
> The glory and peace of that slumber of mine,
> Like a long, gracious rest in the bosom divine!
> The quaint, homely couch, hidden close from the light,
> But daintily drawn from its hiding at night.
> O a nest of delight, from the foot to the head,
> Was the queer little, dear little, old trundle-bed.

The trundle-bed was a common item of furniture in the Middle
Western homestead of the nineteenth century, where families
were large and space was short. It consisted simply of a single bed
with a second mattress and bedding fitted into a drawer which
slid under the main part of the bed. By day, the drawer would be
closed to allow more space in the bedroom; by night, it would be
pulled out to provide a bed.

Mrs. Cook's concern is with recollections of a long-dead
mother; Riley's, with a long past Hoosier boyhood. He slows the
breathless twitter of Mrs. Cook's verse and describes a past lin-
geringly recollected rather than sharply recalled. But, in making
this talismanic quality of the furnishings of "the old home" a
theme of verse, he is clearly treading on Victorian English ground.
Thackeray's "The Cane-Bottomed Chair" is another example of
the same type and in the same comforting jog-trot metre.

This Victorian tendency to poeticize the commonplace details
of life and to imbue them with personal significance, with memory and the hard-won truth of experience, is a common nineteenth-

century American habit. We have only to recall some of Whittier's and Longfellow's popular pieces to recognize that, in this respect, the English and American national psyches had much in common in the late nineteenth century. Longfellow, at least, was as much a Fireside Poet for England as he was for America.

The corollary of this habit of mind is a sense of what we may call "the ubiquity of poesy." For the reader of newspaper and magazine verse in the late nineteenth century, in both England and America, poetry was something that commented on and conveyed wisdom about many aspects of day-to-day experience and about the emotional situations and dilemmas of an average life. Popular poetry was the repository of popular wisdom—a common man's or woman's oracle on how life should be lived. It performed, in fact, some of the functions now alloted to the advice columns of popular journalism.

This rôle of poetry may help to account for the great popularity in Riley's time of an early piece, "If I Knew What Poets Know," a popularity which has not endured. Marcus Dickey records that it was written during Riley's brief period in a law office and that it was one of the poems he sent to Longfellow in 1876 with a letter seeking advice and encouragement.[15] In spite of its comparatively inept phrasing, the poem is a statement of the popular Victorian idea of poetry as a source of wisdom and consolation:

> Where I found a heart in pain
> I would make it glad again;
> . . . . . . . . . . .
> And the world would better grow
> If I knew what poets know.

With youthful modesty, the poet disclaims any healing power in his own work while asserting the consciously ameliorative function of poetry to gladden the heart, even if, as a result, "the false should be the true." In other words, poetry can rose-tint the harsh picture of reality until it is falsified, if the deluded reader is gladdened by the finished picture. Because of this view, it is possible to distinguish at once the source of the appeal of popular poetry to the late nineteenth-century audience and the cause of its wholesale rejection by later generations. The falsity and over-sweetness at the heart of popular verse in the latter half of the nineteenth century effectively killed the popular muse for the twentieth century. Poetry acquired a reputation for softness which it is apparently in no danger of losing. Edgar Guest's newspaper verse, which achieved considerable popularity with a certain type of reader in the 1920's and 1930's, continued the tradition of the popular poet as source of the wisdom of familiar experience. But Guest's work represents this tradition drained even of that vitalizing contact with native American humor which Riley's "philosophical" dialect pieces possess. Guest was the pale successor of a relatively distinguished line of popular poets, as Elbert Hubbard was a late and uninspiring survivor of the robust tradition of rustic humor.

The newspaper poet in the age of popular poetry was, in short, expected to provide the spiritual tempering of an advice column as well as the vicarious emotional experiences and humorous footnotes on life that might be thought of as more naturally his province. The strain this placed on his abilities must at times have been very considerable, and we find Riley apparently near to breaking under it during the time when he was establishing his name on the *Indianapolis Journal*. "O my friend," he writes in a letter of 1880, "if you only knew how they exasperate me—these people I work for and who pay so little—and how exacting they all are—and how everybody wants theirs to be better than all the others—and how little time they have to wait—and how I have to jump from dirges and dead marches to jingles and jimcracks, etc., world without end." [16]

In these circumstances, it may seem surprising that so many of Riley's occasional verses should have had as much contemporary life as they did. One poem of condolence, "Away," was much admired in its time. Its combination of consolations for the bereaved with simple faith in the hereafter is, for its time, remarkably free from cloying sentiment:

> I can not say, and I will not say
> That he is dead.—He is just away!
> With a cheery smile, and a wave of the hand,
> He has wandered into an unknown land,
> And left us dreaming how very fair
> It needs must be, since he lingers there.

The poem, originally a Memorial Day commemoration, first appeared in the *Indianapolis Journal* for May 31, 1884. Like the equally popular dialect piece "The Old Man and Jim," its intent was the consolation of the survivors of Civil War dead; later lines speak of the dead man: ". . . loyal still, as he gave the blows/Of his warrior strength to his country's foes." In edited versions, using the opening and closing lines only, the poem is frequently printed today on cards intended to be sent to bereaved persons. Unlike most of Riley's nondialect poems, with the exception of some of the children's verse, this one poem, which is very much a typical message of condolence of its time, has not dated too much and still conveys an acceptable sentiment.

## IV   *The Obituary Laureate*

The same cannot be said of Riley's numerous patriotic and obituary tributes which he produced more frequently from the 1890's on, as the role of "people's laureate" became more securely his own. A much admired patriotic poem was "The Name of Old Glory." This had first appeared in the December, 1898, number of *Atlantic Monthly,* which had only once before printed a Riley poem and did not print another. "The Name of Old Glory" was a considerable success, however, and its publication in the *Atlantic* represented for its author the attainment of the last citadel of literary reputation. It became another of Riley's popular recitation pieces, and a comment in the *Indianapolis Journal* in 1899 suggests his style as public laureate: "His gestures in reciting this heroic poem are a marvel of grace. Two simple movements of his arms illustrate the waving of a flag from the halyards in a remarkably impressionistic manner, and another and equally simple movement limns the outlines of the flag as it droops. . . . There is a peculiar quality to his voice . . . that really thrills, a quality that actually inspires patriotism." [17]

Riley later recited this poem at the dedication of the monuments on Shiloh battlefield and on other patriotic occasions; for, by the 1890's, Riley was a well-established speaker at banquets and official functions. With the success of "The Name of Old Glory," he was frequently called on to write and recite obituary tributes. He read "The Home Voyage," a tribute to General Henry W. Lawton, who fell at the battle of San Mateo, at the unveiling of a statue of General Lawton in Indianapolis; and his poem "William McKinley" was read at the dedication of the McKinley Memorial in Canton, Ohio. On both these occasions President Theodore Roosevelt spoke.

Riley took very seriously his role of obituary laureate, and he rarely missed the occasion to write a testamentary ode or sonnet when a particular hero or close friend died. But his tributes to Longfellow, President Benjamin Harrison (who had been a close friend of Riley in his early years in Indianapolis), General Lew Wallace, Henry Irving, Lee O. Harris, Eugene Field, and numerous others are no better than the usual versified obituaries; they seek fitting phrases for the occasion but achieve no larger statement.

Yet another form of neo-Victorian verse is found in the once very popular "Lockerbie Street." The form could best be described as the "urban pastoral," and there is nothing else like it in Riley's work except its very poor sequel "Lockerbie Fair." There are not, indeed, many examples in nineteenth-century poetry of the concept of the city as a place of serenity and harmony. Wordsworth's "Westminster Bridge" sonnet is one glowing example, and Arnold's "Scholar Gypsy" makes the city of Oxford a part of the pastoral harmonies of its surrounding countryside.

Riley's use of the idea is on a level altogether different from these examples. Its jog-trot metre and bouncing tone owe more to Eliza Cook than to the English Romantics, and the theme is more that of an island of pastoral pleasure in the "clangor and din/Of the heart of the town" than of the city itself as a place of harmonious contentment. Riley had written the poem in 1880, thirteen years before himself taking up residence on Lockerbie Street. At this time, the street was not in fact part of the city but a suburban development in the process of absorption. Riley deliberately burlesques his theme by overstating his "rhyme-haunted raptures," and the phrases used are typical of contemporary love-poetry:

> . . . the nights that come down the dark pathways of dusk,
> With the stars in their tresses, and odors of musk
> In their moon-woven raiments, bespangled with dews,
> And looped up with lilies for lovers to use
> In the songs that they sing to the tinkle and beat,
> Of their sweet serenadings through Lockerbie Street.

Noting the date of the poem, we may consider it to be an early attempt by Riley to find a pastoral mode acceptable to urban or semiurban taste. Its use of alliteration and light consonantal sounds is, like the phraseology, more typical of some of Riley's love lyrics. As the quoted lines demonstrate, it was a poor thing; but it was popular. Riley did not attempt to develop this form, and it does not appear to have offered much scope for development. His other adventures in pastoral are almost entirely in dialect and derive their subject matter from far different sources.

## V  *The Victorian Dialect Poets*

Riley's use of dialect does not supply any evidence of debt to the Victorian English dialect poets. Tennyson's Northern Farmer and William Barnes' Dorset rustics speak dialect that a Middle Westerner would find extremely difficult to read and to understand. The Northern Farmer—Old or New Style—is an altogether more real creation than Riley's musing semi-illiterate rustic. The harsh Lincolnshire dialect is matched by a harsh sense of social realism—of the duties of the old-style farmer in a rigidly ordered society or the energetic opportunism of his new-style successor. Hard toil and hard bargaining are not a part of the Hoosier pastoral world.

The Dorset farmer is much more the spiritual brother of the Hoosier farmer of Riley's Middle Western pastorals. He has the same sense of serene independence—"I got two vields, an' I don't ceäre/What squire mid have a bigger sheäre." [18]—the same nostalgia for a happy past—

> In happy days when I wer young
> An' had noo ho, and laugh'd an' zung,
> The maid were merry by her cow,
> An' men wer merry wi' the plough.[19]

—and the same sense of the consolations of family ties in alleviating the stings of time:

> The bloom that woonce did overspread
> Your rounded cheäk, as time went by,

A-shrinkèn to a patch o' red,
    Did feäde so soft's the evenèn sky:
The evenèn sky, my faithful wife,
O' days as feäir's our happy life.[20]

To offset these striking similarities of tone and feeling, there are, however, notable differences. Barnes is a much more descriptive poet, and in poem after poem—"The Evenen Star O' Zummer" is an example—he creates a pastoral scene almost as a painter creates a canvas of closely observed detail. And the social milieu of Barnes' *Hwomely Rhymes* (1859) and *Poems of Rural Life in the Dorset Dialect* (1862) is a different world from that of Riley's *Neghborly Poems* and many later volumes. The innocent peasants of Barnes are of the same blood as John Clare's and Thomas Hardy's peasants, rooted in the soil they work and a part of the nature they move in. Riley simply does not describe the Indiana scene often or closely enough to merit serious consideration as a nature poet. His humor and pastoral sentiment are essentially expressions of character, and his characters are pioneers, or their children, with a stronger sense of the claims of family and community than of the soil.

As early as 1888, a collection of Riley's poems, *Old-Fashioned Roses*, was published in England by Longmans and Co., as a result of Charles Longmans' being "very much taken with J. Whitcomb Riley's poems" while on a trip to America in that year, as reported in the *Chicago Herald*. The collection had some success; a second edition appeared in 1891; the book remained in print until 1928, and it was last reprinted in 1912. A birthday book of Riley quotations, *The Golden Year*, appeared in London in 1898; and some of the later American volumes were sold in England by Longmans.

It cannot be said, however, that Riley achieved, or sought, a British reputation. He did not, apparently, attempt to publish his work in British magazines. On his visit to Scotland and England in 1891, his chief purpose seems to have been to visit the birthplace and the last home of Burns, though he also took the opportunity to renew old acquaintances in London. He gave a reading in the Beefsteak Room of the Lyceum Theatre for Irving, Constant Coquelin, Bram Stoker and other distinguished guests. Irving, along with Ellen Terry, had been captivated by Riley's reading of "The Old Man and Jim" a few years previously in New York, and Irving apparently pursuaded Riley to repeat the performance at a dinner he gave for him at the Savoy. But there was no question of Riley's achieving the same popular acceptance by the London public as Twain and Artemus Ward had at their public readings. Despite the fact that Riley in his nondialect poems borrowed many elements of style from popular Victorian versifiers and despite the immense vogue in Victorian England of the American Fireside Poets, who appeared in ornate English editions alongside Wordsworth, Tennyson, and Milton, there was little in Riley's particular brand of sentimentalized humor to exert any strong appeal to English popular taste in the 1890's.

Since the "Victorian" aspect of Riley is perhaps the least known to modern readers, I have quoted generously from many pieces which may not appear to merit extensive discussion. As the quotations have indicated, Riley, in his nondialect verses, genre pieces for the newspapers and magazines, is generally working at the level of what Newton Arvin called "masscult poetry"—"A kind of cheaply-manufactured, as it were machine-produced 'poetry'— newspaper verse, domestic doggerel, rhymes about miners and prospectors and the like." [21] He was writing "for market," and we may choose to adopt the castigating tone of Roy Harvey Pearce and place him in the lowest level of nineteenth-century American poetry (lower than the "élite" poets, "Emerson and his kind," and lower than the Fireside Poets, who strove to write for a truly popular "middle" audience) with "Mrs. Sigourney and her kind who, lacking the intelligence to assume their proper responsibilities, catered to and exploited the general (or generalized) reader." [22] But the situation would not have been so interpreted by the more socially elevated of Riley's "general (or generalized)" readers. For them, particularly for "the middle-class readers (mostly women) of the *Atlantic Monthly*," [23] the pieces in Hoosier dialect were the lowest form of current poetic art, a form without edification or the "lift" of a truly literary style. Riley's success in establishing himself as a writer of "correct" English, as well as of dialect, played an important part in his popular acceptance.

Although in his dialect pieces Riley was working within an established and fertile American tradition, critical opinion was slow in accepting the validity of this tradition but Riley in his turn was not slow to assert his claim to propriety as a writer of "literary" poems in approved diction. As such, he was one of a host of minor American poets and novelists of the period who strove "to preserve the sweeter morals and records of the Republic and worked to transplant those of Victorian England." [24]

CHAPTER 5

# The Child-World

IT MIGHT appear on first consideration that James Whitcomb Riley's talent, with its penchant for themes of nostalgia and the recollected past, was not especially adapted to the writing of verse for children. For the child, the past is only beginning to exist; if it has any meaning, it means only the previous day. The future is the unknown, peopled with adult myths and far-sounding glories. The present, perhaps because it is all there is, seems limitless, so that life becomes one endless day, punctuated by sleep.

So also the child's relative lack of a sense of place, of the here and there, can make an infinity of the finite. The most unimaginative child can invest commonplace reality with a sense of wonder. The most ordinary street, house, tree, or garden can become for him a place of enchantment by the kind of instant personal mythologizing which he can practice at will. Even if the materials of this mythology are derived from the poorest sources, there is a seeming permanence to the dimension of amazement in which the child sees the real world. As this sense is dulled by experience, where once everything was new, nothing is new. The dimension of imagination becomes memory or the future, and the present is merely real.

Much of James Whitcomb Riley's "adult" verse is the expression of a nostalgia for an idealized rural America of pioneer and early postpioneer times, of simple people and honest, uncomplicated values. It was perhaps inevitable that Riley would be drawn to writing children's verse about the rural childhood he had known in Greenfield, Indiana; and it is perhaps not surprising that, of the great quantity of verse of this type which he produced, only a handful of the children's poems are at all familiar to younger readers today. The idealized rural past of the adult poems is of a piece with the idealized present of the child poems; but, where the world of the adult poems can be irritatingly folksy and overly picturesque, that of the child poems is a more convincing reality since it is one selectively remembered, as most of us remember our own childhood—a place of permanent sunshine, boisterous enjoyment and, on the whole, of kindly people, a never-never land where we have been but cannot come again.

Riley's children's verse is collected chiefly in three volumes: *Rhymes of Childhood* (1891), a typical grab-bag of material collected from newspapers and magazines, notably the *Indianapolis Journal* and *Century Magazine;* A *Child-World* (1897), most of which was work appearing for the first time; and *The Book of Joyous Children* (1902), short poems again largely first published here, apart from a few reprinted from *Century Magazine.* The verse as a whole divides into the two familiar genres of children's poetry. The first we may call "genuine children's poems," in which the writer tries to approximate the child's mind—to think through his mind—in the way that Stevenson does in poem after poem of *A Child's Garden of Verses.* Riley, who devoutly admired Stevenson, even wrote a poem to accompany a photograph of Stevenson as a blond young man,[1] but he does not often attain Stevenson's level.

Much more often Riley writes poems of the second category, for "children of all ages"—poems about children which can be enjoyed, or are more likely to be enjoyed, by adult readers. In these he recreates the recollected world of childhood, partly by evocative descriptions of its external circumstances, but much more by reproducing the dialect speech of the Hoosier child. This can be so skillfully done, as in "The Bear Story," that the poem becomes a true children's poem, one which children recognize as an authentic expression of their thought as they would think it.

Children understand far more than they can express; and, though they have an instinctive narrative sense, they frequently have trouble with details and with the sequence of events. In such poems as "The Bear Story," Riley recreates the stumblings, circumlocutions, false starts, and gropings for expression of the average child telling a story in a way that children can readily enjoy. In other poems—"Maymie's Story of Red Riding Hood" is one of these—the reproduction of child speech is too exact. We grow irritated by the lisping coyness, and so presumably do children, since this poem was never a children's favorite.

## I   The Book of Joyous Children

The children's verse, like the "adult" verse, is in both dialect and modern English; and, as usual with Riley, his best and most characteristic things are in dialect. There are, however, some successful efforts in modern English, though the effects are often imitative. We may consider the poems of *The Book of Joyous Children* first since, as a whole, they are intended for the youngest ones, nursery-age children; and they can perhaps be more readily enjoyed by children than the earlier published pieces.

There is the usual variety of styles. "An Impromptu Fairy Tale" is a dialect version of the doings of fairyland, at once a delightful debunking of the more fey variety of fairy poems for children, and a comic picture of what the Hoosier child can make of a fairy story:

> Wunst he blowed an' telled 'em all:
>     "Saddle up yer bees—
>     Fireflies is gittin' fat
>     An' sassy as you please!—
>     Guess we'll go a-huntin'!"
> So they hunt' a little bit,
> Till the king blowed "Supper-time,"
>     Nen they all quit.
>
> Nen they have a Banqut
>     In the Palace-hall,
> An 'ist et! and 'et! and 'et!
>     Nen they have a *Ball;*
> An' when the *Queen* o' Fairyland
>     Come p'omenadin' through
> The King says an' halts her,—
>     "Guess I'll marry you!"

In such poems as "No Boy Knows," Riley attempts to create that sense of the mystery of ordinary things which Stevenson creates in poems like "The Land of Counterpane" and "The Land of 'Nod" and which Walter de la Mare was later to perfect in poem after poem. We have only to juxtapose some lines of "The Land of

Nod" with some from "No Boy Knows" to see the great gulf fixed
between Stevenson and Riley as children's poets.

Stevenson:

> All by myself I have to go,
> With none to tell me what to do—
> All alone beside the streams
> And up the mountain-sides of dreams.
>
> The strangest things are there for me,
> Both things to eat and things to see
> And many frightening sights abroad
> Till morning in the land of Nod.[2]

And here are Riley's more sentimental mysteries:

> O I have followed me o'er and o'er,
> From the flagrant drowse on the parlor-floor,
> To the pleading voice of the mother when
> I even doubted I heard it then—
> To the sense of a kiss, and a moonlit room,
> And dewy odors of locust-bloom—
> A sweet white cot—and a cricket's cheep—
> But no boy knows when he goes to sleep.

Other poems are on familiar topics of the Victorian children's
poet. "Find the Favorite" records a child's delight in the intelligence of cats; "The Boy Patriot," with its refrain "I want to be a
soldier," is a ubiquitous theme (see Stevenson's "Marching Song"
and "Armies in the Fire" for markedly different versions); "Extremes," a slight piece about a very noisy boy and a very quiet girl
which has become a favorite with anthologists, is in the style of
"rhymes for little ones" produced by such earlier nineteenth-
century English writers as Jane and Ann Taylor, the Lambs, Jean
Ingelow, and Mrs. Anna Laetitia Barbauld. "Thomas the Pre-
tender," although it is in dialect and has a hired man in it, is
really another Victorian piece about a boy who pretends to be a
rooster crowing on the fence and falls in the attempt, the moral
being "Tom can't crow but he can cry." "The Katydids" is more
authentically near to home in its description of a boy falling

asleep while trying to decide if the chirping of katydids is their praying, singing, or talking. "Little Dick and the Clock" is an unjustly neglected piece of considerable verbal invention and great charm about a sick boy, alone in his bedroom, who imagines that the clock is talking to him and who tries to understand what it says, until it finally talks him to sleep.

Though Riley never attains that easy but fully convincing transition into the other-world of imagination which is the great merit of Stevenson's poems, he does in a few poems demonstrate something of Stevenson's faculty of transforming the ordinary, easily recognizable experiences of childhood into imaginative experiences which the child can enter into. He frequently relies, as Stevenson does not, on heavy rhythms and repeated sounds or refrains, which may make no particular sense, but appeal to the young child's ear. The "Raggedy Man" poems provide some familiar instances of this.

Thrown in with the mixed bag of *The Book of Joyous Children* are two medleys. "A Session with Uncle Sidney," a miscellany of verses for young and old, includes a Wordsworthian blank verse narrative about the experience of a father and two boys who find a litter of young foxes while out hunting and take them home to care for them. Despite all their efforts, the cubs die and "for long weeks afterward"

> . . . we boys, every night, would go to the door
> And, peering out in the darkness, listening,
> Could hear the poor fox in the black, bleak woods
> Still calling for her little ones in vain.

"Some Songs After Master Singers" is a group of imitations of Shakespeare, Robert Herrick, Wordsworth, Tennyson, Browning, and William Morris. They are never more than barely competent, but they may serve as an indication of the company in which Riley saw himself. The Hoosier rhymester here is in intent the Victorian poet of children.

## II  Rhymes of Childhood

*Rhymes of Childhood,* chronologically the first of Riley's books for children, is a quite varied collection in form and style; but it is about equally divided between dialect and modern English. The author apparently felt it necessary to defend the use of dialect in a prefatory note:

> In presenting herein the child dialect upon an equal footing with the proper or more serious English, the conscientious author feels it neither his desire nor province to offer excuse. . . .
>
> It is just and good to give the elegantly trained and educated child a welcome hearing. It is no less just and pleasant to admit his homely but wholesome-hearted little brother to our interest and love.

The range of styles covers the lyric, narrative, sentimental, and nonsensical. There are some imitations of Tennyson in "The Dream of the Little Princess," of the Lambs in "The Land of Thus-and-So," and of George Macdonald in "The Man in the Moon." We may wonder why Riley did not reprint in this collection the poem called "The South Wind and the Sun" which had appeared in *Afterwhiles* in 1888. An early try at the Stevensonian manner, it is Riley's most successful effort in this vein. This idyll of a summer's day employs the language and fancy of the Victorian children's writer—"the kine, in listless pause, switched their tails in mute applause"—but the nature described is the Middle Western thrush and bobolink, melons, winesap, kildee and rambo. Riley's attempts to people the Middle Western scene with English fairy personages are never completely successful, but there are many felicitous touches of description, such as the "bridled and reined" bees in "waxen stalls that oozed with dews" and the dragonfly "tilting down the waters in a wild, bewildered flight."

But the best of the *Rhymes of Childhood* are the dialect pieces, and a few of these fit the definition of true children's poems. They present us with a view of reality entirely as a child might conceive it, with the drastic limitations of a child's experience and the exuberant stretch of a child's imagination. An amusing example is the favorite anthology piece, "An Impetuous Resolve," about a boy who thinks up careers for his friends as sailor, tailor, and carriage-maker and for himself as a baker. He has resolved these careers into a vision of adult activity which will unite them all forever:

> An' Dick'll buy his sailor-suit
> O' Hame; an' Ham'll take it

An' buy as fine a double-rig
  As ever Bud kin make it.
An' nen all three'll drive roun' fer me,
  An' we'll drive off togevver,
A-slingin' pie-crust 'long the road
  Ferever an' ferever!

This piece, for all its slightness and absurdity, has a hint of the quality of fable which makes certain nursery rhymes immediately appealing and memorable to the child's mind; but it is, given its time and place, an entirely possible thing for a child to imagine.

The best and best-known instances of Riley's ability to create characters of fable for children, are, of course, the poems about the Raggedy Man and the Hired Girl, most of which were collected in *Rhymes of Childhood;* and to these we must add the even better-known "Little Orphant Annie." The first thing to note about the Raggedy Man, who is in fact the Hired Man, is that it is his raggedness, which would make him unattractive to adult eyes, that makes him a figure of romance for the child. We are given a child's-eye view of the adult world, and the child habitually makes heroes of what are thought of as the humbler workers, the postman, bus-driver, baker's man, milkman, or, in Riley's rural world, the hired man. For the very young child, the humbler activities are a source of wonder while the more elevated activities—of business, education, or whatever—are meaningless or uninteresting. So "The Raggedy Man" becomes a catalogue of the marvellous, ordinary things the Raggedy Man can do, which are "most things 'at boys can't do," culminating in the boy's decision that he is "go' to be a nice Raggedy Man" rather than "a rich merchunt" like his father.

There is just a hint of bourgeois condescension in this attitude, the same condescension that Riley occasionally shows in his verses about illiterate farmers. The adult reader is presumably intended to smile indulgently, as the "rich merchunt" father would. But this condescension is no more than hinted, since the child's quality of hero-making is genuinely presented and since the Hired Man is an authentic character, a man of great resource. Apart from his general capability and kindliness, he has the capacity for energetic nonsense which can capture the young child:

> . . . he knows most rhymes
> An' tells 'em, ef I be good, sometimes:
> Knows 'bout Giunts, an' Griffuns, an' Elves,
> An' the Squidgicum-Squees 'at swallers therselves!
> An', rite by the pump in our pasture-lot,
> He showed me the hole 'at the Wunks is got,
> 'at lives 'way deep in the ground. . . .

Another of the Raggedy Man poems, "The Lugubrious Whing-Whang," is all about his capacity for nonsense rhyming, and is a little better than most of Riley's attempts at Carroll-style nonsense.

The Hired Girl, the maidenly counterpart of the Hired Man, is a creature of infinite resource in the kitchen. In "The Hired Girl," the first stanza of the poem is a fond description of her skill in making custard pies. This poem also introduces the other sustaining matter of interest to the young child, the courtship of the Hired Man and the Hired Girl, which is to be developed in the narratives of *A Child-World,* Riley's next book of children's verse. But the basic form of "The Hired Girl" is the ballad rather than the sustained narrative; the characters are, in a child's sense, ballad heroes; and the swinging rhythms and chiming refrains have the same appeal to the child's ear that these qualities in the Border ballads have for listeners of all ages. There are other beginnings of the more developed milieu of *A Child-World* in some of the other poems of *Rhymes of Childhood.* Noey Bixler, one of the boy heroes of *A Child-World,* appears in "The Pet Coon," and Bud, who represents the young James Whitcomb Riley, appears in "The Old Hay-Mow."

Before discussing the later volume, however, it is necessary to comment on the undoubtedly best-known of Riley's child poems, "Little Orphant Annie." For some reason Riley did not reprint this poem in any of his collections for children. It was a relatively early piece, had first appeared as "The Elf Child" in the *Indianapolis Journal* in 1885, was collected in *The Boss-Girl,* and gradually acquired its popularity through Riley's use of it in his public readings. In the process, the Little Orphant Allie of "The Elf Child" became the "Little Orphant Annie" who gave the poem its later title. Although not again collected until the Biographical edition of 1913, it enjoyed great popularity as an anthology piece, as a song in a number of different musical settings, and as a separate illustrated edition.

The orphan child of the poem was a real one who had stayed with the Riley children for a short while in Greenfield. In 1915, the year before Riley's death, she was rediscovered, now Mrs. Wesley Gray, living on a farm not far from Greenfield. She remembered her stay at the Old Homestead; but, ironically enough and remarkably for a Hoosier citizen, she had read nothing of Riley's work. Visitors to the Old Homestead in Greenfield today are shown the "rafter-room, an' cubby-hole, an' press" that are presumably the originals of the ones in the poem. Although the details of the poem, "kitchen fire" and "lamp-wick" are dated now, the invocation of childish terrors and the swing of its movement still exert their appeal for children.

In several respects "Little Orphant Annie" is not typical of Riley's children's poems. Its didactic quality—you must behave or the goblins'll get you—is very untypical in spite of the fact that many of his adult verses are full of lessons about the value of a good heart. Moreover, little girls in general are not much a part of the Riley world; boys and youths are far more in evidence. Little Orphant Annie is, in fact, a little girl lost. She comes into the household from the outside world to "earn her board-an'-keep" and brings into the usually sunny world of Hoosierdom her sense of the strangeness and terrors of the other world of fairyland. The "witch-tales" that she tells, of "two great big Black Things" who snatch the wicked child through the ceiling, have a fascination that holds the childish imagination, just as they do for the children of the poem. The vigorous rhythm and banging refrain appeal to the ear, and the sense of night's terrors when the "moon is gray" produce for the very young child a kind of juvenile *frisson*.

## III  A Child-World

If the best of the *Rhymes of Childhood* can with some justice be claimed as genuine children's poems, the same cannot be said of the narrative pieces in *A Child-World*. Yet, in some respects, this collection is the most satisfying and in every sense the most fully integrated of all of Riley's books. This volume is the only one with a unifying structure; and, were it not for the too frequent passages of pedestrian verse, this sequence of poems might have the same enduring charm as a genre picture of early American rural life that Whittier's "Snow-bound" has.

The structural frame of *A Child-World* can, from a purely technical point of view, be compared with Longfellow's *Tales of a Wayside Inn* (collected in 1886), which may well have provided Riley with the idea for his book. A group of characters is introduced, described in a prologue, and placed in a situation where each tells a story for the others' entertainment. Narrative links between the stories sustain a continuing "real" story which is initiated in the prologue. Riley's aim is to recreate "the Child-World of the long-ago." The setting is the Riley family home in Greenfield—

> A simple old frame house—eight rooms in all—
> Set just one side the center of a small
> But very hopeful Indiana town—
> The upper-story looking squarely down
> Upon the main street, and the main highway
> From East to West,—historic in its day,
> Known as the National Road. . . .

The flatness that mars much of the verse is already apparent, but visitors to Greenfield recognize the authenticity of the scene. The prologue is a loving, lingering description of the sights, sounds, and furnishings of the Old Homestead.

The characters of the "five happy little Hoosier chaps" who first make their appearance are Riley himself and his brothers and sisters—"Jonty, the oldest," is his elder brother John; "his little tow-headed brother, Bud," is the poet as a boy; "Maymie, with her hazy cloud of hair," is his sister Elva May; "Alex . . . affectionate beyond the average child" is his brother Alex; and "baby Lizzie" is his sister Mary Elizabeth. Seven uncles and one aunt, besides the mother and father, comprise the family picture. Uncle Mart, storyteller supreme, is the most important of these; and later Cousin Rufus, a young student of law, appears, along with some neighborhood boys, chief of whom are Almon Keefer, a literary lad of rich imagination, and Noey Bixler, the supremely dextrous boy who can do almost any practical thing.

A family visit to Noey Bixler's house provides the frame for the series of narratives, interspersed by songs, which follow, as the guests in old-fashioned rural style entertain one another. Preluding these is the rustic episode of "The Hired Man and Floretty," whose flirtation is begun here and picked up again in the links between the stories. A secondary romance is that of Cousin Rufus and Miss Wetherell, which finally augurs well after he serenades her on the flute. Somewhat apart from the other characters is "The Noted Traveller," never named, a passing stranger who stays for the night and tells a harsh tale of the hardships of runaway slaves which is apparently intended to temper the bland charm of the overall picture of familial contentment.

The core of the book is provided by the three tales told by children—"Maymie's Story of Red Riding Hood," "Bud's Fairy-Tale," and "The Bear Story that Alex 'ist maked up his-own-sef'." Each of these is a tour de force in dialect blank verse; and, though the results are uneven, Riley's attempt in these three poems to recreate the language and thought of the child telling a story is a notable achievement in an untried form. In fact, the three tales steadily improve from first to last. "Maymie's Story of Red Riding Hood" does not add much to the original, and its lisping artfulness is hardly to the modern reader's taste:

> . . . Nen old Wolf smile
> An' say, so kind: "Where air you doin' at?"
> Nen little Red Riding Hood she says: "I'm doin'
> To my Dran'ma's, 'cause my Ma say I might."

"Bud's Fairy Story," a distinct advance, depends upon another confrontation of the delicate forms of fairyland with the earthier realities of Hoosier rural life. The confrontation can be very harsh:

> An' when I weach to ketch him, an 'uz goin'
> To give him 'nuvver squeezin', *he ist flewed*
> *Clean up on top the arber!*—'Cause, you know,
> They *wuz* wings on him—when he tored his *coat*
> Clean *off*—they *wuz* wings *under there*. But they
> Wuz purty wobbly-like an' wouldn't work
> Hardly at all—'Cause purty soon, when I
> Throwed clods at him, an' sticks, an' got him shoved
> Down *off* o' there, he comes a-floppin' down

> An' lit k-bang! on our old chicken-coop,
> An' ist laid there a-whimper'n like a child!
> An' I tiptoes up rite clos't, an' I says "What's
> The matter wiv ye, Squidjicum?"

Though most of us have never heard children speak in this dialect, the gusto of the action is instantly recognizable as authentic farm boy; and the manner of adapting the blank repetitions of a child's speech is extremely skillful.

"The Bear Story that Alex 'ist maked up his-own-sef' " was the great contemporary favorite of these dialect blank-verse stories and became a popular recitation item. The storyteller is a much younger child, and every step of the narrative is liable to become a false one. The story concerns a little boy who went into the woods to shoot a bear and eventually succeeded after many misadventures, but the story hardly matters. It is the child's excited rendition of it that furnishes our amusement; the words continually tumble over themselves until he must backtrack to make a correction or resume the true line of the story.

The difference in ages between the three storytellers is conveyed in their words and phrases alone, without any extraneous description. Alex's vocabulary is very limited; he has to rely on a few simple phrases to convey his meaning. But where Bud, as an older boy, approaches the fairy world in a spirit of practical and rather heavyhanded exploration, Alex's attitude to the world of adventure is all wonder and wild surprise. With his limited vocabulary, he can convey his sense of wonder only by repetition in the highest key:

> . . . An' when
> The Little Boy he saw the *grea'-big Bear*
> A-comin', he 'uz badder skeered, he wuz,
> Than *any* time! An' so he think he'll climb
> Up *higher*—'way up higher in the tree
> Than the old *Bear* kin climb, you know.—But he—
> He *can't* climb higher 'an old *Bears* kin climb,—
> 'Cause Bears kin climb up higher in the trees
> Than any little Boys in all the Wo-r-r-ld!

Riley is indeed writing for "children of all ages" in these three dialect stories in blank verse. As recreations of the psychology of children at different ages they amuse the adult reader by their truth to life, while there is enough incidental fun in the sudden surprises and problematical twists of the storytelling to amuse a child. But it must be admitted of *A Child-World* as a whole that this verse cannot be recommended for children's reading. The difficulty of reading the dialect alone is considerable, and the movement of blank verse usually escapes the child's ear, so that Riley's subtle rendering of the cadences of children's speech tends to be lost. Kenneth Grahame in the preface to his anthology *The Cambridge Book of Poetry for Children*[3] lists the forms he intentionally omitted, and they include blank verse and all verse in archaic language and dialect. He was, he said, "reluctant to confuse a child's often painful acquirement of normal spelling." The difficulties with many of Riley's dialect pieces are such that they really need to be read aloud by a skillful reader before they can be enjoyed by a child, but with this reservation the potentiality for enjoyment they contain is considerable.

About half of *A Child-World* is in modern English, for the most part in iambic pentameter couplets of the broken variety Keats used in "Endymion." Since Riley is not at his best in this form, the general effect is a little ponderous; and there are some dull pages. But, despite these limitations and the fact that only "The Bear Story" can be said to have survived in any real sense, *A Child-World* is the only one of Riley's volumes that can be recommended as almost continuously pleasant reading. The inescapable sentimentality of the late nineteenth century is present in the exchanges between the young lovers, but with a light touch, avoiding the mawkishness and solemn, inflated diction of most of Riley's literary love poems. The dialect sections are skillfully varied and, because they are largely spoken by children, are without the musing folksiness of Riley's more "philosophical" dialect verses for adults.

There is little chance of resurrecting *A Child-World* as a children's classic. It is not poetry in any absolute sense of the word, and it does not draw any reserve of spiritual strength from the commonplace as Whittier's "Snow-Bound" does. It is an extended genre piece by an artful versifier; but, if the reader does not demand too much of it, he may find that it has not entirely lost its charm as a loving evocation of the more pleasant aspects of rural, family life in the America of almost a century ago.

CHAPTER 6

# The Hoosier Poet

IN spite of considerable critical and popular opposition to dialect verse in the second half of the nineteenth century, it was as the "Hoosier" poet that Riley won his great popular fame and only in this aspect that he appears today to have any individuality or distinction as a poet. His work in "modern English" is, with few exceptions, on a level of third-rate poetastry which appears to offer abundant justification for the customary judgments of the period as one in which "literature, especially poetry, was marked by decline";[1] "poetry, apart from Whitman and Emily Dickinson, was derivative and conventional";[2] and "popular culture was overwhelmingly 'a repetition of given facts'."[3]

The few exceptions in which Riley rises above the generally low level of his "modern English" poems are pieces which most nearly approximate the style of the dialect poems—in a sense, they are dialect pieces without the dialect: simple rural vignettes in plain style. Examples are the brief elegy "When Bessie Died" (which begins to approach the moving understatement of Ransom's "Bells for John Whiteside's Daughter" until it is ruined with a fervidly pietistic final stanza) and the very popular pastoral "Out to Old Aunt Mary's." The latter poem is discussed in some detail in a later chapter, and it must suffice here to say that no great claims can be made for it.

In seeking to exempt Riley's work in dialect, at least in part, from the wholesale condemnation which the bulk of the poetry of the Gilded Age has received, it should be emphasized at the start that the dialect poems do not, any more than those in literary English, rise above the "repetition of given facts." They are no nearer the level of Pearce's "high art" or "élite art," one which "through an initial commitment to fantasy (insight) seeks so to conceive of reality as at least to redefine or enhance it, at most to transform it and 'make it new'—produce a new reality."[4] The

"Hoosier" poetry is no different in its essential subject matter, just as much a presentation of simple moral lessons, the basic platitudes of the good life, and the tender sentiments of courtship and family life. What makes the difference is the mode of presentation. It will be necessary to provide some preliminary definitions of the forms of the dialect poems.

## I   *Form in the Dialect Poems*

The poems in Hoosier dialect may first be divided into those which are narrated and those which are "in character." Both are in dialect, but in the first kind there is a narrator who describes "from outside" the actions of one or more rural characters. The latter may have lines of dialogue ("speak in their own words"), but they do not shape the interpretation of the poem and point its lesson, which is left to the narrator. In some poems, particularly such lyrics as "Nothin' to Say" and "The Old Man and Jim," we learn nothing of the character of the narrator; the message comes across, as it were, without interference. In other poems, most notably in "The Rubaiyat of Doc Sifers," the narrator himself is one of the characters; his qualities are contrasted with those of the character or characters described in the poem.

The poems written "in character" are a distinct group. These are the "Johnson of Boone" poems and a few others in which the character *is* the poet; and the poems are presented as the work of a semiliterate rustic "persona," whose reflections and emotions are thus presented "from within." He makes his own statement of philosophy and his own interpretation of himself. As a result, the amount of dialect in the two basic forms of dialect poems tends to vary. The poems "in character" are rougher in language and form. There is a deliberate crudity in the way a stanza is constructed or a phrase is formed which is part of the humor. In the "narrated" poems, these roughnesses are frequently smoothed out; the effects sought are more often pathos, or narrative swiftness and point. There is humor as well, but it is likely to be mingled with sentiment and different in kind from the comic semibuffoonery of the "Johnson of Boone" poems.

Roughly speaking, we may say that the "narrated" poems are of two types. The first is the "situation poem," most commonly on themes of parting or bereavement, such as the previously mentioned "Nothin' to Say" and "The Old Man and Jim." The second is the "rural narrative," of which there are numerous examples on a wide range of themes, many humorous and sentimental (such as "Farmer Whipple—Bachelor," "What Christmas Fetched the Wigginses," or "His Pa's Romance"), many conveying the moral lessons of experience (for example, "Armazindy" and "How John Quit the Farm"), and a few comic-ironic treatments of defects of character (such as "Scotty" and "Sister Jones's Confession"). The poems "in character" may have a lyric or narrative frame, but all deal with rural or rustic themes and are basically pastoral in type.

The broad divisions which I have outlined serve as a basis for the discussion of particular examples of each type later in this and the next chapter. In general, it may be said that each type is concerned with the presentation of "character" in an almost seventeenth-century sense, but the range of types presented is narrower than that attempted by a John Earle or a John Stephens. The qualities of character emphasized are loyalty, simplicity, "horse sense," persistence, humility, acceptance, and all-around "goodness," the charitable service of humanity. There is little sense of human evil, but envy and jealousy occasionally play a part in the narratives.

In the "situation poems," the response of character to a given situation is presented. In the narratives, character is involved (and sometimes developed) in action or in response to a series of circumstances. In "The Rubaiyat of Doc Sifers," Riley attempts the complete presentation of character, an entire attitude to life. The Middle Western pastorals also do so but in comic or mock-heroic terms. If the moral type or the moral lesson was the raison d'être of the Hoosier poems, for the reader of today it is the sheer entertainment of the narratives that gives them what life they have. As Wallace Stegner puts the matter, "along with a grasp of the plain emotions of common people (or stereotyped emotions of stereotyped people), Riley had a wit, an aptness of phrase, an acuteness of observation that give his work, for all its conventionality, a frequent lift." [5] An assessment of the effectiveness of these qualities is attempted in the analysis of representative examples of the dialect poems. As a preliminary to this analysis, some observations are in order, however, about the prevailing critical and popular attitudes toward dialect poetry at the beginning of Riley's career and about the particular sources of Riley's dialect styles.

## II  *Sources of the Dialect Verse*

The poet's own distinction between "dialect" and "serious work" in a letter to Howells has already been noted. We may suspect that it is an act of deference to the severer standards of the East, but other letters do not bear this out. A letter to Benjamin S. Parker, dated August 29, 1887, on the subject of dialect verse, quotes the issue of *Art Interchange* magazine for August 13 on the subject of Riley's "Nothin' to Say," which had appeared in the August *Century.* The unnamed critic considers that the poem "is an illustration of the only possible excuse for this sort of work" in that "the tender and touching little poem does not depend on the dialect," for "the feeling, the homely pathos of the verse makes it of value, and the dialect is simply its strongest and most fitting expression." Riley's comment is—"Now I am very proud of this detailed estimate of the poem. That is the highest praise I seek or my ambition desires." [6]

This same poem was one of those chosen for the New York readings of 1887. Marcus Dickey notes that "In reciting it, it was said, the poet gained the approval of the entire audience. The silence was intense with applause. Both men and women manifested deep emotion. This was a victory for dialect verse." [7]

In spite, or perhaps because, of the prevailing attitudes, Riley took very seriously his work in dialect. A letter to Lucy S. Furman (yet another aspiring poetess who had sent him some dialect sketches) of February 14, 1893, tells her:

> The field you have found is splendid, and your sincerity in recognising in it the real worth of such simple, homely material is a splendid sign as well. Therefore, do not glean it carelessly, but with elaborate pains. In dialect be as conscientious as in your purest English—seeing to it always, with most vigilant minuteness, that your unlettered characters are themselves in thought, word and deed. In your lettered introductions, descriptions and interludes use all the masterly arts at your command, but in their thought, action, language and the rest, remember no vaguest betrayal of the author's presence must be seen or felt. . . . If anything be not plausible as Nature, reject it—scratch it out. The work must appear positively veracious—in the true artist's mind it is fact, whatever he may fashion of the material. . . . Never—

on penalty of *death!*—must any word not in the vocabulary of the
unlettered be used. Their vocabulary must do their speaking, in
its place.[8]

And he goes on to a long list of correct dialect usages—"not 'till'
but 'tel'; not 'been' but 'ben'; not 'ought' but 'ort'; not 'took' but
'tuck'; not 'held' but 'helt'; not 'early' but 'airly'," and so on.

Riley was certainly sincere in his advice, and his obsessional
concern with accuracy of dialect spelling became matter for le-
gend with his publishers—"one 'get' for 'git' would prove fatal to
me, as you know," [9] he writes in a letter to Bill Nye when asking
for proofs of *Nye and Riley's Railway Guide*. Riley believed that
he was doing a valuable work in preserving the forms of Hoosier
speech, and he would have supported Lowell's view that "No language after it has faded into diction, none that cannot suck up the
feeding juices secreted for it in the rich mother-earth of common
folk, can bring forth a sound and lusty book. True vigor and
heartiness of phrase do not pass from book to book, but from man
to man." [10] In a letter to Thomas Wentworth Higginson of December 9, 1891, Riley devotes considerable space to justifying the
use of "thist" for "just" as "a localism obtaining back into my
remotest childhood memories." [11]

His most complete statement, almost a manifesto, on the subject is the essay "Dialect in Literature," which first appeared in
*The Forum* for December, 1892, and which was collected in the
1895 edition of *Neghborly Poems* [Riley's spelling]. In this article
Riley defines dialect as "any speech or vernacular outside the pre-
scribed form of good English in its present state"; and he asserts
that "its origin is oftentimes of as royal caste as that of any
speech." Dialect can be as effective in literature as "speech and act
refined" because it is "simply, purely natural and human." In the
literature of his own time, "The Lettered and Unlettered powers
are at swords' points." There is hostility and resentment of patronage. "One knows the very core and centre of refined civilization,
and this only; the other knows the outlying wilds and suburbs of
civilization, and this only. Whose, therefore, is the greater knowledge and whose the just right of any whit of self-glorification." He
then appraises the work in dialect of his American contemporaries.

The dialect tradition in verse, though securely founded, was not

of very long duration in American literature when Riley began to
utilize its forms in the 1870's. Hamlin Garland, as a young columnist for the Boston *Transcript* and a public lecturer in the 1880's,
was greatly interested in the subject of the dialect tradition. He
included Riley's work in his lectures on "Vernacular Literature"
after it had attracted his enthusiastic attention following the publication of *The Old Swimmin' Hole* in 1883. Garland believed
that there had been no attempt at recording common speech until
"the first hint . . . in James Fenimore Cooper," but in Cooper's
work "only now and again does the speech of the characters ring
true." This was "not so much a lack of perception as a lack of
valuations." Lowell in the *Biglow Papers* had employed dialect for
polemic purposes and in "The Courtin' " had produced "an enduring genre picture of Colonial life, a charming idyl which has truth
and loveliness." Whittier in his second period "wrote beautifully
of Massachusetts farm life but made no attempt at representing
the dialogue of his neighbors"—"He caught the spirit but not the
accent of his region," except in "Skipper Ireson's Ride," where the
dialect is Irish. Oliver Wendell Holmes, in "The Deacon's Masterpiece," "How the Old Horse Won the Bet," and a few other poems
presented real scenes but only a few words of dialect.

"The vernacular of the toiler," in Garland's view, appeared first
in the newspapers and later was reported in the stories of travellers." The first real appearance in verse was in Bret Harte's work
of the 1870's. Such poems as "Dow's Flat" and "Jim" "faithfully
recorded the speech of the Western man," and Harte had "no
predecessor in this attempt to present actual men and their accent." John Hay's volumes of 1871 consolidated the new style.

To Hamlin Garland, "Unimportant as these poems of Harte and
Hay may appear today, they were immensely significant of a new
country, a new freedom and a changing people." In Riley's book,
he states, "I found the verses all written from the standpoint of an
Indiana farmer, and utterly unlike any other I had read. Here
were subjects no-one else had ever used." [12]

Although there are certain gaps in Garland's record, he was no
doubt right in playing down the influence of Harte and Hay in
Riley's dialect verse; but the verse of the 1883 volume does not
represent the full range of Riley's dialect styles. There is little of
the exaggeration, the under- and overstatement, and the comic
inversions of Harte's verse in Riley. Harte's poems have the kind

of legendary or phenomenal quality of the typical frontier yarn, a string of remarkable events (cf. "Dow's Flat"), and he often favors a kind of unlettered formality, a ponderous gobbledegook which was not in Riley's style. Examples are legion but these lines from *Plain Language from Truthful James* may suffice:

> Ah Sin was his name;
>     And I shall not deny,
> In regard to the same,
>     What that name might imply;
> But his smile it was pensive and childlike,
> As I frequent remarked to Bill Nye.[13]

Harte's influence was more apparent in Riley's prose sketches, but there are a few poems which show Riley trying out this style along with the rest. One of these is "Tugg Martin":

> Tugg Martin's tough—no doubt o' that!
>     And down there at
> The town he come from word's bin sent
> Advisin' this-here Settle-ment
>     To kindo' *humor* Tugg, and not
>         To git him hot.

Tugg is "wanted back there" as a horse thief and eventually, while enjoying a game of cards in the saloon, he is called outside by a deputy. Before long, Tugg returns, handcuffed, to resume the game:

> Yit smilin', like he hadn't bin
> Away at all! And when we ast him where
> The *Deputy* wuz at,—"I don't know *where*", Tugg said,—
>     "All *I* know is—he's dead."

We are in "Tugg Martin" some way from the genial Hoosierdom of the majority of Riley's dialect verses. "The Way It Wuz" also upsets the usual picture of small-town content in a description of an unforgettable fistfight between "Dock" and "Mike" which the narrator alone witnesses, because

> I wuz the on'y man aroun'—
> (Durn old-fogey town!

> 'Peared more like, to me,
> *Sund'y* than *Saturd'y!*).

There is also little suggestion of an influence from John Hay's dialect poems in Riley's work. The punching ballad metre of Hay's "Jim Bludso"—

> The fire bust out as she clared the bar,
> And burnt a hole in the night,
> And quick as a flash she turned, and made
> For that willer-bank on the right.[14]

—is one form Riley does not attempt. Jim's sense of his duty to his fellow men is a Hoosier virtue, but it would not there be a matter of "trust in his cussedness." The child-hero of Hay's "Little Breeches" sets out "Hell-to-split over the prairie" behind a runaway team and when he is found—

> . . . thar sot Little Breeches and chirped,
> As peart as ever you see,
> "I want a chaw of terbacker,
> And that's what's the matter with me."

The children of Riley's child-poems would have been as shocked by his "chaw" as their mothers, and there is no indication in Riley's work that he would have appreciated the narrator's no-nonsense note at the conclusion of "Little Breeches" on the angels who have saved the child—

> And I think that saving a little child,
> And fotching him to his own,
> Is a derned sight better business
> Than loafing around a throne.

One discernible influence in Riley's dialect verse which Hamlin Garland overlooked was that of Will Carleton's *Farm Ballads*. These had appeared during the late 1860's and early 1870's and were collected in 1873. Their dialect is, however, much more "tidied up" than Riley's. Their typical form of slack *aabb* stanzas is much like that of the "Johnson of Boone" poems. Their narrative movement is generally slower than that of Riley's rural narratives, there is much less of the cut and thrust of dialogue and argument than Riley achieves, but their typical narrative themes of tender sorrow, nostalgic regret, and simple undemanding happiness are very like those Riley employs.

In some respects, Carleton's treatment of his subjects is more "realistic" than that of Riley, who is less willing to depict human ugliness and meanness. Carleton's "Betsy and I Are Out" records the decision of a long-married farm couple to part after a petty quarrel. "How Betsy and I Made Up" describes their realization that they want to stay together, though prying neighbors and the "ancient virgin" who wants "to kindle another fuss" do not make it easy. "Johnny Rich" is the tale of a village drunk who always wins forgiveness, another semirealistic piece; but "Out of the Old House, Nancy" presents the kind of sentimental regard for the pioneer past that Riley repeated endlessly, yet Carleton's grasp of the emotional realities of this state of mind is perhaps more true to life than Riley's. The situation in "Out of the Old House, Nancy" is that of a couple who are "moving from the old loghouse" after nineteen or twenty years to a fine new house—

And I won't go back on it now, or go to pokin' fun—
There's such a thing as praisin' a thing for the good that it has done.[15]

The narrator recalls the hardships and happiness of the pioneer life and decides that "There's precious things in this old house we never can take away." In a Riley poem, there would never have been any doubt of it. "Gone with a Handsomer Man" presents the possible pain and sorrow of married love in a realistic manner, but Carleton's final twist of the story to provide a happy ending with the realization that "it was all a mistake" is more typical of Riley's narratives of courtship and love's troubles.

It is, therefore, not strictly accurate to apply to all of Riley's dialect verses Hamlin Garland's encomium that they were "utterly unlike any other I had read—Here were subjects no-one else had ever used." [16] In the situation poems and in the rural narratives, at least, he was dealing with known material; but his treatment of it was everything—especially suited to platform presentation—and Riley's abilities in this respect were testified to by authorities from Irving on. Hamlin Garland, for example, comments on the audi-

ence's response to the New York readings of 1877: "With his first
line he woke that tired audience. There was something at once
human and dramatic in him. He had humor and pathos and the
quality we call magnetism, and he also possessed the art of the
true comedian. As they used to say of English actors, 'the pit rose
at him.' " [17]

### III   *The Situation Poems*

"Nothin' to Say" was one of the hits of this occasion. The situation is that of an old widowed man whose only child, a daughter,
has told him that she wants to be married. He is full of regret, but
he has "nothin' to say" against her wish. The coming parting with
the daughter is compared with the mother's death—

> You look lots like yer mother; purty much same in size;
> And about the same complected; and favor about the eyes:
> Like her, too, about livin' here, because *she* couldn't stay;
> It'll 'most seem like you was dead like her!—but I hain't got
>      nothin' to say!

The mother and he had "run away" when she "was jes' twenty," so
that the present occasion for sorrow becomes one for recollected
joy, for regret, for pride, for a hint of anger (since the child's will-
fulness, the cause of his sorrow, is like her parents'), and for the
pathetic acceptance of the old that life is with the young and must
pass the old by. The old man stoically accepts the loneliness that
life has dealt him. The mingling of emotions, of tenderness and
strength of character, makes the piece a challenge to the actor,
who is aided by several histrionic touches—

> You don't rickollect her, I reckon? No, you wasn't a year old
>      then!
> And now yer—how old *air* you? W'y, child, not *'twenty'!* When?
> . . . . . . . . . . . . . . . . . . . .
> Twenty year! and as good a gyrl as parent ever found!
> There's a straw ketched on to yer dress there—I'll brush if off—
>      turn round.

The emotions are built into the monologue and so are the opportunities for conveying them by intonation, pause, and gesture.

This poem is "in character"; the emotions are in the dialogue. In "The Old Man and Jim," another very popular platform piece, the emotions are narrated, still in dialect; but the subject is again the situation of parting and of regretful pride. In this poem, the parting is that of the old man's son Jim for the Civil War. His words of parting become the refrain—"Well, good-by, Jim:/Take keer of yourse'f." As the narrative is developed through an account of Jim's first leavetaking for camp, his bravery in his first battle, his heroism "in the calvery" and his return after the war, with ". . . the glorious old Red-White-and-Blue/A-laughin' the news down over Jim"—the refrain is repeated and each step in the narrative becomes a situation of parting until, at the conclusion, Jim dies of wounds with "His father's, the old voice in his ear,—/ 'Well, good-by, Jim:/Take keer of yourse'f.'"

Riley presents a simple countryman's view of the Civil War. We are told nothing but the attitude of the old man and his son to the war and to the son's part in it. The mingling of emotions is one of regret and pride. The old man's pride in Jim is partly a matter of self-pride ("likin' him all to hisself like, see?"), until ultimately pride must conquer regret in the final parting. Self-pride in one form or another and the stoical acceptance of the loneliness of old age are the qualities stressed in these two poems. They are typical examples of Riley's treatment of the pathetic, in which the sentimentality is frequently tempered with a stronger mood. Neither poem is particularly happy, though each is positive in its dominant tone; the reader or auditor receives a moral shot in the arm. Riley could treat the subject of old age, and particularly the character of the old man, in other ways, but these examples serve to illustrate that bland geniality is not always his predominant attitude toward these themes.

## IV  *The Rural Narratives*

In many of the rural narratives, sheer fun, with more or less of sentiment added, may be the poet's main intention. Present pleasures rather than recollected joys become the subject, and whatever pathos there is generally derives from the pangs of young love. "What Christmas Fetched the Wigginses" shows Riley in his best vein on the subject of rural courtship. Characteristically, much of the happiness is contrived. The successful culmination of an apparently hopeless young love coincides with Christmas. The narrator, a farm boy of twenty, is the only son in a dull household; and the first lines set the audience and the scene:

> Winter-time, 'er Summer-time,
> Of late years I notice I'm,
> Kind o' like, more subjec' to
> What the *weather* is. Now, *you*
> Folks 'at lives in *town*, I s'pose,
> Thinks it's bully when it snows;
> But the chap 'at chops and hauls
> Yer wood fer ye, and then stalls,
> And snaps tuggs and swingletrees,
> And then has to walk 'er freeze,
> Hain't so much 'stuck *on*' the snow
> As stuck *in* it—Bless ye, no!

The skill with which Riley can use the fast-moving seven-syllable trochaic couplets to convey the natural flow of dialogue is considerable. This brief example, with its fill-ins, emphases, and slow build-up to a point, is typical of the natural effect Riley strove for.

The boy, bored with life in his home, finds a lot more entertainment at the Wigginses. The picture of winter boredom is sketched in with skillful economy and no false note:

> Nothin' round *our* place to keep
> Me at home—with Pop asleep
> 'Fore its dark; and Mother in
> Mango pickles to her chin;
> And the girls, all still as death,
> Piecin' quilts.—Since I drawed breath
> Twenty year' ago, and heerd
> Some girls whisper'n' so's it 'peared
> Like they had a row o' pins
> In their mouth—right there begins
> My first rickollections. . . .

The Wigginses are by contrast a bright and colorful family; the boys—"Price, and Chape, and Mandaville,/Poke, Chasteen, and 'Catfish Bill' "—and the girl—

> . . . Melviney, sometimes, *she*
> Gits her slate and algebry
> And jes' sits there cipher'n' thue
> Sums old Roy hisse'f cain't do!—
> Jes' sets there, and tilts her chair
> Forreds tel, 'pear like, her hair
> Jes' *spills* in her lap—and then
> She jes' dips it up again—

and "old Roy"—

> F'r instance, start the old man on
> Huntin' scrapes, 'fore game was gone
> 'Way back in the Forties, when
> Bears stold pigs right out the pen,
> Er went waltzin' 'crost the farm
> With a beehive on their arm.

Riley creates, without cloying sentiment, a picture of farm life emphasizing its real joys and depicting through young eyes as adventure and fun the hardships of pioneer life.

The expected romantic involvement between the narrator and Melviney also avoids sentiment by the rapid movement of a complicated plot. Poke, the young boy and "the beatin'est/Little schemer," deceives Melviney by means of forged notes into thinking she has a beau; but she declares that she loves another. The narrator, who has long loved Melviney in silence, wrings the story out of Poke and listens with a sinking heart until he is told that the "other man" is himself and that Poke has arranged the wedding for Christmas. This is sentiment, but it charms rather than cloys, and is perhaps "real," at least in a twenty-year-old's view of reality.

"A New Year's Time at Willards's" is a slightly more adult treatment of a similar theme. In it, the opposition to the courtship of a hired man and a farmer's daughter comes from the wealthy old farmer. The narrative is shared between the "hired man" and the "old man." There are some elaborate turns of the plot before the old man is won over, and some deft sketching in of character, such as this version of the old man by the hired man:

> Well, now, old Willards hain't so bad,
> Considerin' the chance he's had.
> Of course, he's rich, an' sleeps an' eats
> Whenever he's a mind to: Takes
> An' leans back in the Amen-seats
> An' thanks the Lord fer all he makes.—
> That's purty much all folks has got
> Ag'inst the old man, like as not!

That all should turn to sweetness at the end may make these narratives into genre pieces, but it should not be allowed to obscure the accuracy and frequent wit of Riley's character drawing, nor the skill with which his dramatic turns of plot are managed. These vignettes of farm life are a miniaturist's art, but considerable artistry has gone into them; and there is more polish to their versification than the dialect form may suggest.

Even at his most didactic, Riley can be entertaining in these narratives of farm life. "Armazindy" is the nearest female equivalent of Doc Sifers as a figure of all-around goodness, but the emphasis is on sheer dogged and cheerful endurance in the face of misfortune. Armazindy Ballenger, the eldest daughter of an orphaned family, is left when "jes' a *child*" to care for the young twins of the family and "her old fittified Grand-aunt." The father had died in the Civil War; and, not unexpectedly, Armazindy is seen as the inheritor of his heroic sense of self-denial:

> And I've heerd her laugh and say:—
> "Jes' afore Pap marched away,
> He says, 'I depend on *you,*
> Armazindy, come what may—
> You must be a soldier, too'."

The mother, who had "allus be'n sickly," does not survive the shock of losing her husband; but Armazindy blossoms under the burden of duty that suddenly falls on her:

> Jevver watch a primrose 'bout
> Minute 'for it blossoms out—
> Kind o' loosen-like and blow
> Up its muscles, don't you know,
> And, all suddent, bu'st and bloom

> Out life-size?—Well, I persume
> 'At's the only measure I
> Kin size Armazindy by!—
> Jes' a *child*, one minute,—nex',
> *Woman-grown*. . . .

But she has the strength of a man and the will to make

> . . . things git up and git
> Round that little farm o' hern!—
> Shouldered all the whole concern;—
> Feed the stock and milk the cows—
> Run the *farm* and run the *house!*
> *Only* thing she didn't do
> Wuz to plough and harvest too.

She has more to endure when the chance of marriage to young Sol Stephens is lost by the wiles of a girl named Jule Reddinhouse, who takes him for herself and then, growing tired of married life, goes off with another man, leaving Sol with their two children. Not long after, Sol, who has taken to drink, dies after an accident with a thresher. He dies in Armazindy's arms; and she, to no one's surprise, takes the two new orphans into her own family.

The outline of the narrative sounds like the tritest piece of Sunday-school tract didacticism, but the poem can be read with the same kind of amused enjoyment we receive from such didactic Wordsworthian efforts as "The Idiot Boy." Everything depends on the telling, and Riley "sugars the pill" with the narrator's little touches of observation of rural life. When Armazindy is left parentless

> (Kind o' grief *I* understand
> Losin' *my* companion,—and
> Still a widower—and still
> Hinted at, like neighbors will!)

—the aside provides a momentary touch of humor which also prepares for the conclusion, when the narrator tells us he has

> Years now . . . be'n coaxin' her—
> Armazindy Ballenger—

> To inlarge her fambily
> Jes' *one* more by takin' *me*—
> Which I'm feared she never will,
> Though I'm 'lectioneerin' still.

The theme is guyed a little in this hint of the humorous side to the catalogue of misfortunes Armazindy has so heroically endured.

Some of the narratives are cloyingly sentimental, and Riley can on occasions wallow in the tear-jerking pathos which appealed to the taste of the age. It is usually the narratives in stanza forms rather than those in brisk couplets (with occasional quatrains to vary the pattern) that expatiate in excessive pathos. "Dot Leedle Boy" is a tear-jerking Christmas piece—the mingling of grief and Christmas is typical of Riley's linking of situations to wring the pathos out of them[18]—that is spoken in the character and dialect of a German immigrant. There are a few poems of this type in Riley's work, and they are indicative of the increasing popularity in the late nineteenth and early twentieth century of immigrant types—Irish, Jewish, German, Scandinavian—in American humor, and of the tendency of these to replace Yankee rural types. This trend becomes noticeable in the theater as well as in humorous writing and is, of course, indicative of an urbanization of dialect humor. The comic immigrant survives strongly into vaudeville, but the comic rustic does not.

Riley's "Dot Leedle Boy" first appeared in 1876 [19] and is a comparatively early instance of this humor type; but it is, however, an exercise in the comic-pathetic. The narrator's simple pride in his son is touching as well as amusing—

> No more he vas older
> As about a dozen months
> He speak der English language
> Und der German—bote at vonce!
> Und he dringk his glass of lager
> Like a Londsman for der Rhine—
> Und I klingk my glass togeder
> Mit dot leedle boy of mine!

When the boy wanders in the snow, falls ill, and slowly dies amid the preparations for Christmas, the comedy of the father's simple pride and the Christmas gifts ("a leedle schmall tin rooster") is blended with grief that wipes out any hint of ridicule in its pathos:

> Der sun don't shine *dot* Gristmas!
>   . . . Eef dot leedle boy vould *liff'd*—
> No deefer-en'! for *Heaven* vas
>   His leedle Gristmas gift!
> Und der *rooster*, und der *gandy*,
>   Und me—und my Katrine—
> Und der jaybird—is a-vaiting
>   For dot leedle boy of mine.

This poem was another popular platform piece, and it aptly illustrates the popular demand for such almost syrupy pathos. But Riley can occasionally be tart and ironic in the narratives, usually in brief, sharp sketches that convey a lot of character in a few touches. In "Scotty," the narrator tells Scotty's story in thirty-four lines; and, in the process, he damns himself as a despairing ne'er-do-well. "Luck liked Scotty mor'n me" is the gist of the account of Scotty's skill and bravery at school and in the war; and, though "Both as pore as pore could be," they have stuck together— "Scotty allus, as I've said,/Luckiest—And now he's *dead!*"

"Sister Jones's Confession" is a twenty-line vignette, etched with acid, depicting a meetinghouse romance through the words of Sister Jones, who ". . . thought the deacon liked me, yit/ . . . warn't adzackly shore of it." Sister Jones had felt doubtful when she had

> . . . seed him shakin' hands as free
> With all the sistern as with me!
> But jurin' last Revival, where
> He called on *me* to lead in prayer
> An' kneeled there with me, side by side,
> A-whisper'n' "he felt santified
> Jes' tetchin' of my gyarment's hem,"—
> That settled things as fur as them-
> Thare *other* wimmin was concerned!

But she is let down lightly at the conclusion as we are given a hint of her simple gladness—

. . . I know I must 'a' turned
A dozen colors!—*Flurried?*—la!
No mortal sinner never saw
A gladder widder than the one
A-kneelin' there and wonderun'
Who'd pray!—So glad, upon my word,
I railly couldn't thank the Lord!

There is not a word wasted nor any suggestion of manipulating the emotion toward sentimentality or pathos in the few Riley pieces of this type.

In one long narrative, *The Rubaiyat of Doc Sifers*, which was published as a separate volume in 1897, Riley attempts a portrait of the "compleat man," the ideal type of simple man dedicated to the service of humanity who combines all the virtues of the Rileyan ethos. Doc Sifers is a kind of Vicar of Wakefield of the Gilded Age, and it is instructive to note that a doctor should represent this type. Sinclair Lewis may, unconsciously perhaps, have drawn on Riley's use of this character in the depiction of the fallible but dedicated hero Doctor Kennicott of *Main Street*.

The *Rubaiyat* started as a short poem of fifteen stanzas, "Doc Sifers," published in 1887. It was added to over the next ten years to make the 105 quatrains of the final poem; and, in the process, the character was completely transformed and idealized. The original Doc Sifers is an eccentric who is likely to be "down at the Gunsmith Shop a-stuffin' birds" when he is wanted; who is full of curious skills and inventiveness; and who is, when he puts his mind to it, a skillful physician and surgeon.

In the later poem, much of the eccentricity is ironed out, and the role of skillful physician is developed in a portrait of the dedicated public servant serving all, yet independent, with a mind of his own, unflurried, patient, wise. The inventiveness is retained, but much of the eccentricity is shifted to the narrator, who reveals himself as a quizzical, "tetchy" old man, often with little sympathy for the ailments of Doc's patients. The idealized Sifers practices service to all, "man er woman, chic er child er team." Some have claimed he was absent-minded and feared to take his medicine because, in preparing it, he seemed to have his mind on something else, ". . . like County Ditch, er some/New way o' tannin' mussrat-pelts, er makin' butter come."

The Benjamin Franklin ideal, combining inventiveness and practicality, may have its shortcomings; but the Doctor always moves among his fellow villagers in a way to edify them. He is "allus sociable, polite and 'greeable"; has a way with horses; is respected by all women; loved by children; is skillful in training dogs; has an abundance of curious lore about stars, "vines and moss," "warter," and "fishin'." He does not claim any creed, "ner raise no loud, vainglorious prayers"; instead, he lives a creed, and his "total faith in Life to Come" has earned him the right to joke about death. He is "feared o' talk," not loquacious; and thus he is the very opposite of Riley's other ideal rural type, the unlettered philosopher of the pastorals. But Doc's repudiation of a "scientific" villager is one of the strong moments of the poem, as the narrator reports it:

> "No, Ike," says Doc, "this world hain't saw no brains like yourn
>      and mine
> With sense enough to grasp a law 'at takes a brain divine.—
> I've bared the thoughts of brains in doubt, and felt their finest
>      pulse,—
> And mortal brains jes' won't turn out omnipotent results!"

The Doctor's inventiveness is elaborated in accounts of his inventions (self-opening stable doors and the like), his adeptness in handling bees, and his skill in giving evidence in court. He favors mercy toward the criminal and stresses the imperfections of law. He "hates contentions" and likes to "see folks agreed," but democratically, "takin' ekal interest and universal heed/O' ever'body else's words an' idies." He is generous to a fault, full of simple patriotism for the flag, and fond of taking hunting trips, which are always followed by generous largesse to his neighbors. Riley falsifies the portrait at the conclusion in indicating it is that of yet another childlike old man: "He's jes' a child, 's what Sifers is. . . ./With perfect faith in God and man a-shinin' in his eyes." The portrait is more complex than the summation indicates, and is finally, in spite of the Franklin touches, that of a secularized man of God, devoted to the service of his fellow man. As a learned and practical man, he complements the type of the ignorant man of simple faith that Riley depicted in the pastorals, the subject of Chapter 7.

### CHAPTER 7

# The Middle Western Pastoral

RILEY'S work in the pastoral form came to represent for his age "the essential Riley" and is, with a few exceptions from the rural narratives, the part most worth preserving of his total *oeuvre*. There are pastoral elements in much of his other work in dialect and even some pastoral poems in modern English. Riley was not above attempting to people the Middle Western landscape with mythological trappings, in such neo-Keatsian sonnets as "Pan," which sees the god loitering

> . . . listlessly by woody streams,
> Soaking the lush glooms up with laziness;
> Or drowsing while the maiden winds caress
> Him prankishly, and powder him with gleams
> Of sifted sunshine.

But this note was not the one to appeal to any but the more fastidiously literary of lady magazine readers. Riley's very popular pastoral "Out to Old Aunt Mary's" is also in modern English; in some respects it suggests Whittier's pastoral manner and calls for more detailed consideration later. Our task for the moment is to establish the setting for the uniquely Rileyan pastorals of 1882, for an extended consideration of these poems has been deferred to this chapter precisely because they represent the essential qualities of Riley's work, and thus an analysis of them profits from a preliminary survey of his work in other forms.

## I  The "Johnson of Boone" Poems

In fact, the "Johnson of Boone" poems were Riley's first published book, *The Old Swimmin' Hole and 'Leven More Poems* of 1883, which helped to establish his growing reputation and which led within four years to the triumphantly successful New York readings. By 1883, however, Riley had been published regularly in local newspapers for something like eight years, had a considerable reputation as a reader of his work, and was a salaried humorous writer for the *Indianapolis Journal*. The pastorals were, therefore, mature work. The twelve poems appeared in the *Indianapolis Journal* between June 17 and September 12, 1882, all being written in the few months following Riley's very successful appearance in Boston in January of that year. Riley's authorship was not acknowledged until the twelfth poem, "The Clover," appeared.

The popularity of these poems with Middle Western readers was immediate, and a collected volume of them was proposed by a colleague on the *Journal* staff, George C. Hitt. When no publisher could be found, a privately published edition, printed in Cincinnati, of one thousand copies appeared in the summer of 1883, the costs being shared by Hitt and Riley. The success of this led to a second edition, published by Merrill, Meigs and Company, of Indianapolis; as already mentioned, this company later became the Bowen-Merrill Company (now the Bobbs-Merrill Company), and Riley's association with it lasted until his death. As we have also previously noted, the association was a close personal one and was astutely managed to the great profit of both parties, which may help to explain why so many of Riley's later books were first published in Indianapolis long after he had published successful volumes with the Century Company of New York and had begun the publication of his collected works with Scribner's. Riley did not abandon his regional origins nor his regional publisher; and there was no particular reason why he should since the regional aspects of his poetic personality had established his national popularity.

Copies of the first edition of the 1883 volume were sent to various writers and critics. Twain was immediately responsive; and his friendship with Riley, never close but always appreciative and respectful, dates from this time. John Hay also wrote his thanks. Robert Underwood Johnson, the editor of *Century* magazine, reviewed the book, stating that he was "very much in sympathy with its substance" but found "a tendency to over-dramatise the close of a poem" and that in several cases he had a desire to draw a pencil through a final stanza. Joel Chandler Harris wrote that

Riley had "caught the true American spirit and flavor." Riley replied gratefully and declared that "The old classic splints are being taken off, as it were, and our modern authors are striking straight out from the shoulder." [1] Hamlin Garland's enthusiastic reaction to the appearance of the 1883 volume has already been discussed.

Riley felt that he was taking off "the old classic splints" in expressing the mood of a pastoral, paradisal yet nostalgic contentment "in character," through the persona of a semi-illiterate old farmer who knows only the present and the recent past of his own immediate locality and whose sense of *eheu fugaces* comes out in this mock heroic form:

> Oh! the old swimmin'-hole! whare the crick so still and deep
> Looked like a baby-river that was laying half asleep,
> And the gurgle of the worter round the drift jest below
> Sounded like the laugh of something we onc't used to know
> Before we could remember anything but the eyes
> Of the angels lookin' out as we left Paradise;
> But the merry days of youth is beyond our controle,
> And it's hard to part ferever with the old swimmin'-hole.

In fact, Riley is adapting some of the traditional elements of pastoral in the classical or European form to an already well-established tradition in American literature and in the process radically transforming that tradition.

## II   *The Pastoral Form*

But, before discussing Riley's pastorals in detail, it is necessary to consider the traditional elements of this form. The pastoralist depicts a society apart from "the world," a rural community in which the simple relationships of members of a family or of young lovers are uncomplicated by and unspoiled by the influences of more "civilized" or urbanized values. William Empson, in commenting on the implication of the "flower born to blush unseen" of Gray's *Elegy*, states that part of the meaning conveyed is that "it is lucky for the poor man that society keeps him unspotted from the world." [2] This antiurbanism, the wish to keep things simple, is omnipresent in Riley's work, where it often takes a comic form, comic-pathetic in "The Old Swimmin'-Hole," for example—

> Oh! The old swimmin'-hole! When I last saw the place,
> The scenes was all changed, like the change in my face;
> The bridge of the railroad now crosses the spot
> Whare the old divin'-log lays sunk and fergot—

or comic-pugnacious in "The Little Town o' Tailholt," that perfect
expression of the anti-Algerism and antiprogressivism which was
one aspect of the Gilded Age—

> You kin boast about yer cities, and their stiddy growth and size,
> And brag about yer County-seats, and business enterprise,
> And railroads, and factories, and all sich foolery—
> But the little Town o' Tailholt is big enough fer me!
>
> . . . . . . . . . . . . . . . . . . .
> You kin smile and turn yer nose up, and joke and hev yer fun,
> And laugh and holler "'Tail-holts is better holts'n none!"
> Ef the city suits you better, w'y, hit's where you'd ort'o be—
> But the little Town o' Tailholt's good enough fer me!

The praise of simplicity which is so basic an element of pastoral
traditionally is expressed in the form of the love of young shepherds and shepherdesses or of prince and country maid.[3] There
are admirable opportunities for burlesque here, which the Restoration dramatists, particularly Wycherley, exploited to the full. Riley, however, takes this element comparatively straight; and his
young pastoral lovers, as we have seen from the discussion of the
rural narratives, are pure and simple, and indeed their love frequently prevails by the strength of its purity and simplicity. This
element also, of vicissitudes overcome by pure love, becomes an
element of comedy—of romantic comedy.

In Riley's pastorals, the quality of simplicity is most strongly expressed in the persons of the old man and the boy, or we might
make a composite old man/boy figure, since nearly all Riley's old
men are boys at heart. The value of the old man as a pastoral character is that he is the repository of older, simpler values. The boy's
values are also simple, but he has the freshness and vitality of
youth. The combination of the two assures a freshness and charm
in the treatment of pastoral themes ("charm" from the boyish
simplicity of the old man's attitude) and also permits the frequent
indulgence of nostalgia. Pastoral gaiety follows its traditional pat-

tern in becoming tinged with an elegiac strain, or in this case with a note of nostalgic melancholy.

The traditional comic figure of pastoral is, of course, that of the boor or clown, whose natural roughness and clumsiness contrast with the natural sweetness and elegance of the shepherds and shepherdesses. As Empson notes, this character can provide the source of the satiric or didactic element in pastoral, in the conventional relationship of prince and clown. "The simple man," Empson states, "becomes a clumsy fool who yet has better 'sense' than his betters and can say things more fundamentally true; he is 'in contact with nature,' which the complex man needs to be." [4] If, for the relationship of prince and clown, we substitute that of city man and country man, we are in the world of Riley's pastorals and in a position to determine the kind of relationship with his audience which the poet establishes in these poems. In writing for the newspaper of a large Middle Western city or for the lecture platforms of the larger cities throughout the United States, Riley adopts in these poems the persona of a pioneer rustic. Pioneer days were then only some fifty years in the past; although the audience of the 1880's had achieved a measure of progress, it was not far, therefore, from its pioneer origins. The effects of the Benjamin F. Johnson persona were thus flattering (you have achieved more sense), reassuring (your roots, so near, are sound, are "in contact with nature"), and reanimating (the sense of nature's plenitude which the clown enjoys can be shared).

That other traditional element of pastoral, the sense of independence, of freedom from the demands of "the world," is also present in the Riley pastorals. Many of the poems are solitary reflections. But, in fact, the ties of family relationship and family love are never far away; therefore, this independence is a safe one, reassured by the presence of family loyalties.

In seeking to define the American tradition of pastoral in which Riley develops the Middle Western form (for it is his innovation), we may briefly consider first the work of two other practitioners of dialect who were contemporary with Riley—Twain and Joel Chandler Harris. In Twain's *Huckleberry Finn* (1885) and Harris' *Uncle Remus* stories (1883 and later) we have a boy and an old man who both "speak in dialect" and who are both for their authors a means of conveying truth artlessly and in such a manner that we have no cause to suspect their interpretations of life. Such simple characters have nothing to gain and nothing to lose. Twain satirizes the crudities of frontier culture (in the furnishings of the Grangerford home), of the Southern code of honor (in the feuds of the Grangerfords and the Sheperdsons), and of the double standard of morality which condones slavery (in Huck's naïve reactions and troubled self-questionings concerning these things), but Harris drives home the fabulist's eternal lessons of human cupidity, vanity, and treachery in the old slave's animal tales. In both cases the source of the interpretation of life and of the advice —which is a matter of "reading into" their tales the simple moral truths they expose—is gently mocked by the author.[5] But the validity of their interpretations is not in doubt. Both are simple souls in touch with the truth because they are near to nature.

Riley's Benjamin F. Johnson is no less "a simple soul in touch with the truth," but his antecedents are somewhat different. Both Huck and Uncle Remus are individual creations, though they are also subdued versions of the folk hero. Huck, a kind of latter-day Bumppo, is independent, uncommitted except to his own code of natural values, which are not those of civilized society and especially not those of "the frontier" that is after all only civilization impinging on the wilderness. Uncle Remus is a source of folk wisdom, the folk being the subject race of Southern civilization. But there is not in Harris the same "play" as in Twain between "civilized" and "uncivilized" values, except on the elemental level of the fable. Benjamin F. Johnson, as a character type, derives somewhat more directly, with less individuation, from the folk figure of the crackerbarrel philosopher, who is traditionally in American literature a source of hard sense, however much of a buffoon he may become. T. C. Haliburton's Sam Slick shows him at his most sensible.

Jennette Tandy has described the origins of this type as follows: "Every age, every country has its imaginery representations of the boor, the clown, the peasant and the small bourgeois. Such groups of portraits often grow into recognized character types or are taken over by men of letters after a long existence in popular anecdote."[6] Some of these types are comic; some express "a personification of the folk," a type "whose tricks and misfortunes, homely wisdom and shrewd observations on the life about him are given a certain moral, social or political significance." "Such a folk hero, the homely American," Miss Tandy continues, exists "behind a certain group of American character types. . . . With wise saws and rustic anecdotes and deliberately cruel innuendo he interprets the provincial eccentricities of American life and the petty corruptions of American political intrigue. Hosea Biglow, Josh Billings, Bill Arp, Mr. Dooley, Abe Martin, are successive incarnations of Uncle Sam, the unlettered philosopher."

Poor Richard, the saw-sayer of the *Farmer's Almanack*, and Jack Downing of Downingsville are other examples of the same type. Moreover, the "rustic" aspects of Franklin and Lincoln are emphasized so that "popular myth makes these men rustic critics, backwoods philosophers, instead of politicians and men of the world." In American literature and the subliterature of newspaper writing, there is a long succession of these personages. They began to emerge from the oral subliterary written tradition about 1830. From 1830 to 1865–67, in Miss Tandy's view, this company made up a body of historically significant political caricatures of some literary merit. During the 1860's and 1870's Josh Billings and Artemus Ward excelled in social caricature. In the 1880's and 1890's, "The unlettered philosopher existed only in minor capacities and a multiplicity of sub-types."

In the most developed form, the unlettered philosopher, the Uncle Sam type, "embodies our sardonic trustfulness, our matter-of-fact idealism, our exuberance and our Puritanism." But it is as one of the multiplicity of subtypes that Benjamin F. Johnson represents the unlettered philosopher, and there is considerable muting of his traditional elements.

### III    *Antecedents in Lowell*

Though Riley claimed to have a poor opinion of Lowell's use of dialect in the *Biglow Papers*, it is in these and particularly in the second series that we find the nearest recognizable antecedent of Benjamin F. Johnson. There is, of course, in Riley nothing of Lowell's polemic intent and none of the biting irony of "Nimepence a day fer killin' folks comes kind o' low fer murder." Nor is there anything of the characteristic Hudibrastic rattle of the Biglow verses—

> I du believe in Freedom's cause,
> Ez fur away as Paris is;

> I love to see her stick her claws
> In them infarnal Pharisees

nor much of Biglow's comically elaborate rhymes. But there is a general resemblance in Biglow's fondness for expressive rustic similes, of which examples are legion—

> Take them editors that's crowin'
> Like a cockerel three months old,

or—

> Wen an Arnold the star-spangled banner bestains,
> Holl Fourth o' Julys seems to bile in my veins,

or—

> Pledges air awfle breachy cattle
> Thet preudunt farmer's don't turn out.[7]

Lowell's "Second Letter From Birdofredum Sawin" (describing "a miles emeritus returning to the bosom of his family" and cataloguing his missing limbs, eye, and fingers) utilizes an apparently traditional tale of a comically mutilated soldier which Riley made the subject of a very popular prose piece in his readings, entitled "The Old Soldier's Story." [8] Twain celebrates Riley's storytelling skill with this yarn in "How to Tell A Story." [9] But Lowell's use of the comic countryman is, of course, as one who "had by rights the ear of many who were deaf to the ordinary appeals of editor and orator. He could insinuate many things forbidden. The rustic observer could innocently betray official double-dealing. He could poke fun wherever he chose, tell all manner of slighting stories about the great." [10] Hosea Biglow does not so much insinuate as shout; and Birdofredum Sawin, in his descent from clown to comic rascal, himself embodies official double-dealing. In the second series of *Biglow Papers,* however, in the picture of pastoral content after martial strife,[11] we see the same softening of the satiric element in the unlettered philosopher that Riley was to develop in the character of Benjamin F. Johnson.

The partnership of Bill Nye and Riley on the reading platform was based on this existence of a hard and a soft aspect of the tradition of the unlettered philosopher. Much of Bill Nye's humor depends on comic exaggeration, but there is some sharp social satire in his sketches of Long Island foxhunting and in his portraits of Jay Gould, "The great railroad swallower and amateur Philanthropist," [12] while he is capable of the Twain-like scorn of this passage: "In this period of progress and high-grade civilization, when Satan takes humanity up to the top of a high mountain and shows his railroads and his kerosene oil and his distilleries and his coffers filled with pure leaf lard and says: 'All this will I give for a seat on the Senate'. . . ." [13]

In their partnership for public readings, Nye presented the satire and grotesquerie of the crackerbarrel tradition, while Riley, in his readings of pieces like "When the Frost is on the Punkin," presented its blander aspects, what Jennette Tandy calls its "matter-of-fact idealism" and "exuberance."

## IV  *The Elimination of Satire*

In Riley's dialect pastorals there is no "innocent" (because "uninvolved") comment on social wrongs and affectations and none of the shrewd, blunt, or ironic social criticism of the crackerbarrel philosopher. Instead, there is the innocence of genial contentment. Thus Riley constructs his dialect pastorals out of materials that are in their origins humorous and satiric. The satire is removed, and the humor lies not in the ironic bite of the rustic philosopher's outspoken comments, but in the simplicity and naïveté of the contented rustic's daydreaming. The crudities of the rustic's utterance are in a sense turned against him and in a sense sentimentalized. They are comic but quaint. The sensibilities of the sophisticated reader or listener are touched rather than shaken by the crudities of utterance. The realism of regional literature is giving place to the charm of the "local-color" school, a shift of emphasis more readily apparent in the contemporary novel.

This shift of emphasis is also clearly the result of a change in taste, itself the result of social change. An amusing illustration of the contemporary social attitude to change is supplied in the description of a large sign painted at South Bend, Indiana, in 1873, by Riley the signpainter:

Its dimensions were astounding. . . . It was a series of pictures apparently in one—"The Contrast of Forty Years"—South Bend in 1833 when a few log cabins stood on the River St. Joe, and South Bend, the prosperous city of 1873. Over against the pioneer, surrounded by the crude implements of his time, stood the man of fortune surrounded by modern conveniences. Left and right respectively, were an ox cart and a Studebaker wagon; a bear and a fat cow; a fur trading post surrounded by Indians and a commercial emporium surrounded by pleased customers; a well-sweep and a gushing fountain; a judge holding court in a shanty by the river and a modern stone court house; a flatboat and a steam boat; a boarding house and a big hotel; a prairie swamp and a Brussels carpet; a stump and a cushioned rocking chair; an ax and a gold-headed cane; the log hut and the palace; a family with no news at all and one with books and the daily paper.[14]

The increasing urbanization and social sophistication of the community were cause for pride, so that there was an element of patronage toward pioneer beginnings in the audience of the 1880's. On the other hand, the living survivors of those early days were still a part of the community. If their ignorance was childlike, it represented the childhood of the community and of the state; and the childlike old pioneer farmer thus became the almost symbolic object of sentimental regard and affectionate respect. The generation of the 1880's wanted to retain and develop the material benefits of the present, but it also wanted to keep the strength of the rural virtues of simplicity and satisfaction with the little that God's bounty afforded for a life of toil—hence the coexistence of the Alger myth and the "Little Town o' Tailholt" view of antiprogress. But the latter was subject for humor rather than for serious exposition, and the Gilded Age took the standard of personal, material success with deadly seriousness. Riley's poems do not so much mock this standard as those who would question it. There is, however, throughout his work, and throughout his life, a note of wistful regret for the lost simplicity of childhood, which can be transferred with no sense of strain to a nostalgia for "the airly days," the childhood of the community.

These preliminary observations on certain changes in the taste of the Gilded Age are necessary if the "Johnson of Boone" pastorals are not to be regarded simply as crude specimens of newspaper humor in verse. Riley plays with great skill upon the mingled feelings of his audience with regard to their pioneer past. We may choose to regard this as manipulation, but Riley himself shared these feelings and had in his own life made the transition from the near-pioneer conditions of Greenfield in the 1850's to the comparative urban sophistication of Indianapolis in the 1880's.

## V  The Comic Persona

The Preface to *Neghborly Poems and Dialect Sketches* (1891), in which the poems of 1883 were reprinted with additional material, sets the attitude toward the persona of Benjamin F. Johnson. The "country poet" is recalled from "as far back into boyhood as the writer's memory may intelligently go"—"He was, and is, as common as the 'country fiddler' and as full of good old-fashioned music." Riley's purpose in "this series of dialectic studies" is "simply . . . to reflect the real worth of this homely child of nature, and to echo faithfully, if possible, the faltering music of his song."

Riley goes on to reprint in its entirety the article "A Boone County Pastoral," [15] with which the series was introduced in the *Indianapolis Journal*. In this article the text of the rustic poet's supposed letters sent to accompany the poems, in the semiliterate style of Petroleum V. Nasby, is set out with editorial comment: "In all sincerity, Mr. Johnson, we are glad to publish the poem you send, and just as you have written it. That is its greatest charm. Its very defects compose its excellence. You need no better education than the one from which emanates 'The Old Swimmin' Hole'. It is real poetry, and all the more tender and lovable for the unquestionable evidence it bears of having been written 'from the hart out'." The second poem is described as "this later amaranth of blooming wildwood verse." This editorial setting of educated comment recalls that of the *Biglow Papers,* except that Riley, unlike Lowell, presents no mockery of the "educated comment" itself.

In "The Old Swimmin'-Hole," the comic crudity of the poet's language, his bumbling metre and the predominant note of nostalgia for "the airly days," should not be allowed to obscure the emphasis on the sense of paradisal innocence in pioneer childhood: "Before we could remember anything but the eyes/ Of the angels lookin' out as we left Paradise." This version of the American Adam as a comic old man recalling his Hoosier boyhood is consistently borne out. Like Whitman's "myself," he is given to solitary reflection and narcissistic reverie:

> Oh! it showed me a face in its warm sunny tide
> That gazed back at me so gay and glorified,
> It made me love myself, as I leaped to caress
> My shadder smilin' up at me with sich tenderness.

But this is a paradise lost, for where

> . . . the bullrushes growed, and the cattails so tall,
> And the sunshine and shadder fell over it all;
> And it mottled the worter with amber and gold
> Tel the glad lillies rocked in the ripples that rolled

there is now a shattered and denuded scene:

> . . . When I last saw the place,
> The scenes was all changed, like the change in my face;
> The bridge of the railroad now crosses the spot
> Whare the old divin'-log lays sunk and fergot.
> And I stray down the banks whare the trees ust to be—
> But never again will theyr shade shelter me!
> And I wish in my sorrow I could strip to the soul,
> And dive off in my grave like the old swimmin'-hole.

The hint of morbidity in the wistful nostalgia, a desire to escape into innocence from the consequences of experience, is also a characteristic of some of these pastorals and perhaps explains Robert Underwood Johnson's desire to "draw a pencil through" some of their final stanzas.

In general, however, the quality of affirmation and the sense of nature's abundance are predominant and make a large part of the rustic poet's humor. The first stanza of "Thoughts fer the Discuraged Farmer" may illustrate this characteristic:

> The summer winds is sniffin' round the bloomin' locus' trees;
> And the clover in the pastur is a big day for the bees,
> And they been a-swiggin' honey, above board and on the sly,
> Tell they stutter in theyr buzzin' and stagger as they fly.
> The flicker on the fence-rail 'pears to jest spit on his wings

And roll up his feathers, by the sassy way he sings;
And the hoss-fly is a-whettin'-up his forelegs fer biz,
And the off-mare is a-switchin' all of her tale they is.

If the drunken bees of the first lines recall Emily Dickinson's
drunken butterflies, the comic picture of Nature as a busy work-
shop in which work gives nothing but pleasure—described with
the typically rustic similes of Josh Billings, Artemus Ward, and
the like—is much more typical of this group of poems. The moral
of "Ort a mortul be complainin' when dumb animals rejoice" is
driven home in a wealth of illustration from farm life:

. . . it's when I git my shotgun drawed up in stiddy rest,
She's as full of tribbelation as a yeller-jacket's nest
. . . . . . . . . . . . . . . . . . .
Does the medder-lark complane, as he swims high and dry
Through the waves of the wind and the blue of the sky?
. . . . . . . . . . . . . . . . . . .
Is the chipmuck's health a-failin'?—Does he walk, er does he run?
Don't the buzzards ooze around up thare jest like they've allus
    done?

There is here, as elsewhere, little distinction between wild nature and the domesticated nature of farm life. In fact, wild nature
has not any "untamed" quality, unless in the marauding bears of
pioneer days. If we may borrow the terminology of Radcliffe
Squire's book on Frost, the quality emphasized is one of "chubby
complacency," and there is no hint of "the impression that nature
is faithful only to herself." [16] Nature has more the quality of faithful friend; and, though the task of subduing it is work, the farmer
of "A Summer Day" can indulge in a reverie of childhood as he
works:

Yit, as I work, I have my fun,
Jest fancyin' these furries here
Is childhood's paths onc't more so dear:—
And so I walk through medder-lands,
And country lanes, and swampy trails
Whare long bullrushes bresh my hands
                . . . I wunder still

> Whichever way a boy's feet will—
> Whare trees has fell, with tangled tops
> Whare dead leaves shakes, I stop fer breth,
> Heerin' the acorn as it drops.

The reader is never allowed to become too serious about the sense of communion with nature, even if the dialect would let him; and the mood is always pushed into humor by a typical "homely" simile:

> Whare pig-tracks, pintin' to'rds the crick,
>     Is picked and printed in the fresh
> Black bottom-lands, like wimmern pick
>     Theyr pie-crusts with a fork, some way
> When bakin' fer camp-meetin' day.

"A Hymb of Faith" is a plain statement of the "Benjamin F. Johnson" philosophy, to "Be more and more contenteder,/Without a-astin' why," with only the faintest hint of the sardonic underneath the simplicity in such lines as—

> They's times, of course, we grope in doubt,
>     And in afflictions sore;
> So knock the louder, Lord, without,
>     And we'll unlock the door.

or—

> O, Thou who doth all things devise
>     And fashion fer the best,
> He'p us who sees with mortul eyes
>     To overlook the rest.

The irony implicit in these last lines is a reminder of the "country poet's" origin in the sardonic and shrewd figure of the cracker-barrel philosopher. But such touches are rare and much more prevalent is the exuberant geniality of poems like "Wortermelon Time," proclaiming the joys of appetite, or "When the Frost is on the Punkin," a comic paean in jingling doggerel for the joys of summer's fulfillment:

> The husky, rusty russel of the tossels of the corn,
> And the raspin' of the tangled leaves, as golden as the morn;
> The stubble in the furries—kindo' lonesome-like, but still
> A-preachin' sermuns to us of the barns they growed to fill.

The "Johnson of Boone" poems are a series of variations on the theme of contentment. In such as "My Philosofy" the contentment is one of accepting the petty meanness of human nature and "doing your best" in spite of it:

> My doctern is to lay aside
> Contensions, and be satisfied:
> Jest do your best, and praise er blame
> That follers that, counts just the same.
> I've allus noticed grate success
> Is mixed with troubles, more er less,
> And it's the man who does the best
> That gits more kicks than all the rest.

"Being satisfied" is not therefore a doctrine of stolid mediocrity; it is one of personal fulfillment which accepts that nothing we do will please everybody and that the better we do, the more some will be displeased. It would obviously be false to equate the overall "moral" of the "Johnson of Boone" poems with the antiprogressive self-satisfaction of "The Little Town o' Tailholt."

In "Wortermelon Time," the contentment is one of enjoyment of nature in its most lush and prodigal mood. In "When the Frost is on the Punkin," another kind of contentment appears in the picture of nature conserving its richness in the "coolin' fall," with "The hosses in theyr stalls below—the clover overhead," the gathered apples, the "strawstack in the medder," the cidermaking over, and the "souse and saussage too." The poem creates a Breughel-like picture of rough and vigorous rural abundance to which the rough and vigorous metre adds the touch of comic rusticity. This picture is not "the only justification" for the dialect form, as the Boston reviewer might have remarked; but it is a natural and appropriate subject for its use. It is also entirely correct in a literary sense, in view of the example of Spenser in the *Shepheards Calender*, which was probably unknown to Riley and possibly also to the Boston reviewer.

There are a few later poems in Hoosier dialect (but without the

semi-illiterate misspellings of the "Johnson of Boone" poems), in
which the lushness and prodigality of the Indiana summer creates
a mood of total laziness—"At Utter Loaf," to borrow the title of
one of them. Two of the most popular of these, "Knee-deep in
June" and "On the Banks o' Deer Crick," were both published in
the *Indianapolis Journal* during 1885. In the first of these, the
sense of Nature's richness is the source of a comic mood of acceptance—

> . . . some afternoon
> Like to jes' git out and rest,
> And not work at nothin' else!

—in which the activity of nature can be appreciated in idleness—

> Pee-wees' singin', to express
>   My opinion's second class,
> Yit you'll hear 'em more er less;
>   Sapsuck's gittin' down to biz,
> Weedin' out the lonesomeness;
>   Mr. Bluejay, full o' sass,
> In them base-ball clothes o' his,
> Sportin' round the orchard jes'
> Like he owned the premises!
>   Sun out in the fields kin sizz,
> But flat on yer back, I guess,
>   In the shade's where glory is!

These poems were never included in the "Johnson of Boone"
series, however. Their exuberant laziness is not of a piece with the
old man's exuberance, which is a sense of the rich rewards of quiet
work, as well as of the openhandedness of nature. The old man's
outlook is also rarely untouched by sorrow, whether of regret that
"the merry days of youth is beyond our controle" or of simple
grief for the dead.

Two of the twelve poems of the original "Johnson of Boone"
series express this simple grief. "On the Death of Little Mahala
Ashcraft" is a kind of rustic foretaste of John Crowe Ransom's
"Bells for John Whiteside's Daughter" and a skillful exercise in the
comedy of bathos:

"Little Haly! Little Haly!" cheeps the robin in the tree;
"Little Haly!" sighs the clover, "Little Haly!" moans the bee;
"Little Haly! Little Haly!" calls the kill-dee at twilight;
And the katydids and crickets hollers "Haly!" all the night.

As in "Dot Leedle Boy," the sense of grief is intended to be aug-
mented by the comedy of its utterance; and it is a purer grief for
being so artless. Riley does not achieve the almost whimsical use
of pathetic fallacy of Ransom's poem, but it is a similar mood he
works towards in lines like these—

And the little Banty chickens kindo' cutters faint and low,
Like the hand that now was feedin' 'em was one they didn't know.

"To My Old Friend, William Leachman" is a tribute to the loyalty of a lifelong friend which also contains a Victorian genre
piece on the theme of sorrow and family grief. The scene of the
burial of "my first womern" is one of the few winter scenes in the
dialect pieces. Again the simplicity of the grief tends towards
bathos, but Riley lifts it above triteness with some realistic
touches:

. . . the snowflakes whirlin', whirlin' and the fields a frozen glare,
And the neghbors' sleds and wagons congergatin' ev'rywhare.
. . . . . . . . . . . . . . . . . . . .
And the clock, like ice a-crackin', clickt the icy hours in two.

The tribute of friendship produces a series of shared recollections
of days in the old settlement which creates the background of the
old farmer as a kind of Founding Father of the community. The
"message" of these poems, that the qualities of the old man are
those on which the community was built, is completed in this
poem.

## VI  *Difficulties of Interpretation*

There are special difficulties in judging a body of verse which
takes the form of the work of a semi-illiterate versifier. It must
obviously be true to the standard of its own semi-illiteracy. Any
attempt to extend the vocabulary or the choice of similes beyond
the limited range likely to the supposed creator would falsify the

verse. In this respect, the "Johnson of Boone" poems succeed admirably. They fulfill Riley's own strict requirements for what is "natural" in dialect verse. But how far must verse of this kind be true to its own ineptitude? When the amateur versifier attempts a literary effect and merely burlesques it, how is the reader to decide whether this is a skillful guying of the versifier's lack of skill or a piece of overwriting on Riley's part that detracts from the "serious" content of the verse, which must, if the poems are fully to succeed, constantly be balanced against the ludicrous aspects?

There are many instances where it is impossible to decide. In "On the Death of Little Mahala Ashcraft," the diction of such a line as "And the katydids and crickets hollers 'Haly!' all the night" can be considered an example of skillful ridicule in that the ludicrous inappropriateness of a word like "hollers" turns towards laughter a situation which calls only for the simple grief the rustic poet feels and tries to express with "art" (in the use of pathetic fallacy), but can express only with the artlessness which is natural to him. But, when later in the poem, we find the following stanza—

> Did her father er her mother ever love her more 'n me,
> Er her sisters er her brother prize her love more tendurly?
> I question—and what answer?—only tears, and tears alone,
> And ev'ry neghbor's eyes is full o' tear-drops as my own

—we may feel that the grief is too plainly stated, the treatment too flat and bald, and the poem is turned toward mawkishness. There is here no comic point to the inept versification; and, since the taste of the age consistently inclined toward the mawkish in its obituary verse, we may suspect that the flatness of the verse in this instance is the fault of Riley, not of his persona.

Almost none of these poems is free from defects of this kind. As another instance, we may cite the concluding lines of "Thoughts fer the Discuraged Farmer":

> Sich fine circumstances ort to make us satisfied;
> Fer the world is full of roses, and the roses full of dew,
> And the dew is full of heavenly love that drips fer me and you.

This phraseology can be taken as the rustic versifier's attempt at the literary, but these concluding lines are the moral of the poem;

they sum up its content, and it may be felt that this serious content is marred by an image of such ugliness. This is, however, a matter of taste; and the fact that these lines became a popular quotation suggests that the taste of the age was moved rather than bothered by an image which may seem overstated and excessive to our own age.

The poems most free from defects of this kind are those, like "My Philosofy" and "A Hymb of Faith," which approach nearest to plain statement, which do not attempt the literary and thus create a sense of doubt as to whose ineptitude is being exposed, the poet's or that of his comic persona. We could argue that the point does not matter, that the verses are meant only to be enjoyed, and that to establish fine distinctions of this sort is to take them too seriously. The distinction, however, is one between the comic and the merely ludicrous. Riley's purpose in this series of poems is the serious one of creating an authentic comic folk hero, as his own statement indicates:

> "Johnson of Boone" has a claim on our respect because he is true to nature. I do not believe in dressing up nature. Nature is good enough for its Creator—it is good enough for me. To me the man Johnson is a living figure. I know what he has read. People seem to think that if a man is out of plumb in his language, he is likewise in his morals. Now the Old Man looks queer, I admit. His clothes do not fit him. He is bent and awkward. But that does not prevent his having a fine head and deep and tender eyes, and a soul in him you can recommend.[17]

In general, it may be stated that, while none of the poems in the series achieves a perfect balance of the comic and the serious, Riley does succeed in creating the figure of Johnson of Boone, largely by the quality of backbone which the poems of plain statement give to a characterization otherwise tending toward an excess of folksy sentiment.

There is also no question that, in this series of poems, Riley set a highly influential precedent in the depiction of farm life and reworked the traditional character of the crackerbarrel philosopher into a substantially different form. In the process, he created what was virtually a new form in American poetry, the Middle Western pastoral, which developed the comic aspects of the New England pastoral (found, for example, in Lowell's "The Courtin'"), avoided its "cultivated" attitudes,[18] and emphasized that tendency in American literature (found especially in Irving and Crevecoeur) toward praise of a settled and abundantly prosperous rural life.

## VII The Example of Whittier

Riley did, however, to some extent work within the tradition of pastoral inherited from the New England poets, primarily from Whittier. There is little difficulty in applying to Riley's work John B. Pickard's general summation of Whittier's literary attitudes: "The best of Whittier's genre pieces and his ballads illustrate the essential truth . . . that underneath the most commonplace objects lay beauty, rich treasures of life's tragedy and comedy. His regional works reveal the inner love of a man for the environment that molded him, the tradition that inspired him and the people that loved him." [19] Riley is perhaps more concerned with the worth than with the beauty of the commonplace, though, in terms of this type of moral thinking, worth is beauty. It expresses the beauty of God's design for mankind.

There are certain similarities in form between Whittier's pastorals and some of Riley's dialect poems, though Whittier actually employs dialect only in "Skipper Ireson's Ride." These similarities do not extend to the "Johnson of Boone" poems, but the octosyllabic couplets of Whittier's "The Barefoot Boy" and "Maud Muller" are frequently the form chosen for Riley's rural narratives, if to different effect. The limpid, even flow of Whittier's couplets and the "cultivated" phrasing of such lines as these from "The Barefoot Boy"—

> Flight of fowl and habitude,
> Of the tenants of the wood
>
> . . . . . . . . .
> Of the black wasp's cunning way
> Mason of his walls of clay,
> And the architectural plans
> Of gray hornet artisans

—these are qualities quite distinct from the brisk, apparently slapdash style of Riley's couplets and his skillful efforts to reproduce the natural cadences of speech. The origins of Whittier's pastoral style are in the tradition of English pastoral stemming from Milton's "L'Allegro" and "Il Penseroso" and their Elizabethan antecedents and maintained through the eighteenth century in such pieces as John Dyer's "Grongar Hill." The origins of Riley's pastoral style, as I have indicated, are in the literature of American vernacular humor and satire.

The exception to this generalization is his poem "Out to Old Aunt Mary's," which might be called Riley's "Snowbound" if it were in any way equal to Whittier's masterpiece. It is one of Riley's very few extensive pastoral pieces not in dialect, and its purpose is to recall "those old days of the lost sunshine/Of youth," as Whittier's is to create "These Flemish pictures of old days" for one "Dreaming in throngful city ways/Of winter joys his boyhood knew." The reason for Riley's choice of modern English is indicated in a note on the poem in the Biographical edition: "My boys and girls are town boys and girls, not children living in the country. They touch the country but are not actually of it. Were they country boys and girls, they would not, as I take it, see any novelty in country life." [20]

The poem was an extremely popular one in Riley's public readings and may be regarded, like "An Old Sweetheart of Mine," as an extended genre piece, this time on the theme of nostalgia for childhood days, and intended for the most "general" reader or listener, one who might be troubled even by the mildly literary flavor of a poem like "Snowbound," with its diction:

> Yet, haply, in some lull of life,
> Some Truce of God which breaks its strife,
> The Worlding's eyes shall gather dew

—and its inversions:

> Or lilies floating in some pond,
> Wood-fringed, the wayside gaze beyond.

There are only the faintest hints of diction and the plainest imagery in "Out to Old Aunt Mary's," while the stanzas move at a comfortable ballad trot completely unlike the stately, melancholy flow of Whittier's couplets, as the following typical stanzas show:—

> The few last houses of the town;
> Then on, up the high creek-bluffs and down;
> Past the squat toll-gate, with its well-sweep pole;
> The bridge, and "the old 'baptizin'-hole',"
> Loitering, awed, o'er pool and shoal,
> Out to Old Aunt Mary's.
>
> . . . . . . . . . . . . . .
>
> And then in the dust of the road again;
> And the teams we met, and the countrymen;
> And the long highways, with sunshine spread
> As thick as butter on country bread,
> Our cares behind, and our hearts ahead
> Out to Old Aunt Mary's.

Riley's poem, like Whittier's, is concerned with the joys of childhood in a farm home; but, where Whittier's poem is so constructed as to separate the limited world of "home," symbolically warmed by the woodfire, from "the world" outside, and to describe "the inevitable impingement of the world upon the quiet of wintry, rural solitude," Riley's poem merely enumerates a number of specific sources of joy, with no attempt to impose a deeper meaning or more universal application on its theme. The joys of food and play—

> The jelly—the jam and the marmalade,
> And the cherry and quince "preserves" she made!
>
> . . . . . . . . . . . . . .
>
> The honey, too, in its amber comb
>
> . . . . . . . . . . . . . .
>
> [The] swooping swing in the locust trees
>
> . . . . . . . . . . . . . .
>
> The talks on the back porch, in the low
> Slanting sun and the evening glow—

are described merely for their own sake and have no deeper significance. Riley is, of course, not a poet of "deeper significances," though there are occasional hints, even in this poem, of an awareness of these, as in these lines:

> And the old spring-house, in the cool green gloom
> Of the willow trees,—and the cooler room
> Where the swinging shelves and the crocks were kept,
> Where the cream in a golden languor slept,
> While the waters gurgled and laughed and wept.

This image of richness extracted and retained within the heat of summer sums up the previous enumeration of pleasures, but it is not developed beyond this. As so often in Riley, joy must end in pathos; and the poem concludes with Aunt Mary's death, though joy to come is assured:

> . . . she waits *today*
> To welcome us:—Aunt Mary fell
> Asleep this morning, whispering, "Tell
> The boys to come" . . . And all is well
> Out to Old Aunt Mary's.

This conclusion simply keeps the poem within the genre category; it is the expected mingling of sorrow with joy and the expected touch of pathos to give the joy an extra "lift." It does not detract from the overall sense of exuberance found as much in this "modern English" pastoral as in Riley's dialect pastorals.

It is this quality that most sharply distinguishes what may be called the Middle Western pastoral from the New England pastoral. In subject matter there are few essential differences. Riley's tale of "barefoot boys in the days gone by," as it were, covers the same ground as Whittier's

> Barefoot boy, with cheeks of tan!
> With thy turned-up pantaloons,
> And thy merry whistled tunes.

But Riley is free of the relentless moralizing of Whittier; he does not contrast the stern and sinful adult world with the innocence of childhood, as Whittier does again and again in such lines as

> Let the million-dollared ride!
> Barefoot, trudging at his side,
> Thou hast more than he can buy
> In the reach of ear and eye—

or the concluding lines of the same poem, with their melancholy picture of a dark future for the barefoot boy, one in which

> All too soon these feet must hide
> In the prison cells of pride
>
> . . . . . . . . . . . .
> Happy if their track be found
> Never on forbidden ground;
> Happy if they sink not in
> Quick and treacherous sands of sin.
> Ah! that thou could'st know thy joy
> Ere it passes, barefoot boy! [21]

The sentiment of Whittier's "Maud Muller" is again totally unlike the typically euphoric mood of Riley's rural narratives in its moral overtones, its melancholy appraisal of the deluded dreams of youth, and its wistful hope that our dreams of happiness may be fulfilled in "the hereafter." In "Telling The Bees" and "Skipper Ireson's Ride," Whittier does not append a moral, but the elegiac tone of the first and the hard lesson of the second are again very unlike the type of treatment Riley might conceivably have given to such subjects.

Riley's work in pastoral form is, of course, full of moralizing, but this is expressed in terms of the moral maxims, the conventionally uplifting sentiments that support the good life. Whittier is just as much a poet of the good life, but his moralizing is tinged with a latent melancholy and an inescapable sense that life is a vale of tribulation in which we can at best hope for interludes of joy. Yet, of all the New England poets, it is Whittier who may most aptly be compared with Riley. The points of similarity with Lowell and Holmes have been previously noted.

CHAPTER *8*

# The Humorous Chronicler of
# Small-Town Life

IN previous chapters we have noted the manner in which Riley
modified and developed certain aspects of the American tradition of humorous writing. By the 1870's the elements of the tradition were well defined. In Lowell's *Biglow Papers* an exuberant
exaggeration of metaphor alternates with a shrewd and wry
understatement. Both exaggeration and understatement are calcu-
lated to set the accepted norm of conduct in a new light and to
impart to the narrator an oracular quality, a tone of sharp common sense heightened with something of the fervor of a revivalis-
tic preacher. Hence the popularity of the lecture platform with
the humorists of the latter half of the nineteenth century. As lec-
turers, they could talk uninterruptedly with an air of authority.
Another common characteristic of these humorists was their appeal to an audience of good plain people, small-town people,
farmers, or city folk who proudly retained the simple, honest,
common sense of their rural forebears.

## I  *Antecedents*

Willard Thorp defines two periods in the development of American literary humor in the nineteenth century.[1] The humorous
writers of the 1830's and 1840's—Seba Smith (in the comic persona of Jack Downing of Downingsville), T. C. Haliburton (Sam
Slick, the Clockmaker), J. R. Lowell (Hosea Biglow, Birdofredom
Sawin)—were essentially regional humorists. They made particular use of the tall story and the practical joke. There was a strong
folk element in their humor, and frequent character sketches of
relatives and neighbors. The humorists of the 1850's and 1860's, on
the other hand, were essentially literary comedians, exploiters of

their own comic personalities in the manner familiar today from the work of radio and television comedians. The humor of "Artemus Ward" (Charles Farrar Browne), "Petroleum V. Nasby" (David Ross Locke), "Josh Billings" (Henry Wheeler Shaw), Bill Arp, and Bill Nye is seldom regional in content and is closely associated with the character of the narrator. Much of it depends on his pithy sayings in comic sketches and burlesque lectures. There are few characters in the work of these writers apart from their own comic personae; and, in expressing these, they relied heavily on the verbal humor of semiliterate spelling and phraseology. They misspelled nearly all their words, partly to indicate pronunciation and partly to show their audience that they were simple, uneducated people of whom no one need be afraid. They employed homely metaphor for the same reason that they misspelled.

Common to the humorists of both periods was their penchant for social criticism, on the largest scale in their biting satire on national policies and big business methods and on a smaller scale in their ridicule of the foibles and follies of individual humble persons. The unifying persona of all these writers emerges ultimately as the cartoonist's "Uncle Sam," essentially a Yankee type, the tall lank figure in high-crowned hat, blue coat, and nankeen striped trousers, who is ageless and vitally alive, who is notorious for his shrewdness and famous for his wit, and whose sharp business sense is concealed under a deep simplicity and an inexhaustible sociability.

Twain retained the elements of the humorous tradition established by his predecessors but informed them with genius. As the "Explanatory" preface to *Huckleberry Finn* implies, the use of dialect becomes a medium for the expression of regional differences and thus of individual character. The satire on national policies, political chicanery, and business skulduggery is deepened and broadened until it ultimately assumes tragic dimensions as an indictment of the essential criminality of fallen man. An exuberant invention of incident and a poker-faced understatement of comment alternate as before. The ridicule of humble foibles produces a rich cast of minor characters, gullible, unscrupulous, crass, wicked, or touchingly simple. There is an added element of nostalgic regard for some lost, archetypal simplicity of rural life, one best illustrated perhaps in the descriptions of the furnishings, decorations, and activities of the Grangerford household in *Huckle-*

*berry Finn.* They are offered without comment, and the reader can
make of them what he will. Crude and comic, they suggest the
lost childhood of a race that has moved on to roistering adoles-
cence and to a young manhood going progessively to the bad.

In Bret Harte, regional humor again emerges. The simple, fundamentally good and heroically enduring soul appears alongside
the inveterate rascal. There is also an increasing concern with the
humor of defeat. His female characters are frequently sentimen-
tally idealized, but to compensate this is the irony that adherence
to the code of the West produces and the satire of biting understatement.

## II   *The Small Town in American Literature*

As we have noted in Chapter 7, Riley's use of the humorous
tradition, partly as the result of temperamental inclination and
partly due to a change in popular taste, is a process of selection
and softening of its elements. In effect, he blends certain elements
of the humorous tradition with those of another stream of American writing, already flowing strong by the latter half of the nineteenth century, the literature of small-town life.

From the third quarter of the eighteenth century, there had developed a body of small-town literature embracing many forms—
poetry, fiction of many types, essays, histories, letters, diaries, au-
tobiographies, and travel sketches. Their writers reflected in varying degrees of realism, social satire, or romantic idealization the
prevailing attitudes toward a widely diversified community life in
the small town, and in the villages and rural environs that provided its reason for being.

The harshly critical side of this body of literature originated in
the painful strictures of foreign travellers on the social life they
encountered on their usually well-subsidized visits to the United
States. From Mrs. Frances Trollope in *Domestic Manners of the
Americans* (1832) to Dickens in his *American Notes* (1842), to
Matthew Arnold in his *Civilisation in the United States* (1888),
the picture that emerges of life in the small towns and villages of
the extending frontier of the Middle West and West is one of
crude, harsh, inelegant, and intellectually frustrating limitation.
These awkward and uncouth people, with their raucous voices,
hard faces, whiskey drinking, tobacco chewing, love for politics,

and harshly restrictive religion were sunk in crudity and ignorance. The borrowed elegance of Boston almost alone provided a haven in which the traveller might feel at home.

The native-born realists—Edward Eggleston in *The Hoosier Schoolmaster* (1871), Joseph Kirkland in *Zury: The Meanest Man in Spring County* (1887), Edgar Watson Howe in *The Story of a Country Town* (1883), and many other novels by these and other writers—continued the assertion of the crudity of material life, the ugliness of manners, and the poverty of imagination of the small towns of the Middle West and the West, but with a different motivation. The travellers were concerned with recording and generalizing upon impressions often hastily arrived at, which took no account of the fact that the communities they had seen were merely at an early stage in the evolution of a rapidly developing country. The provincial realists did not evade the coarseness and ugliness of the life they described, but they regarded that life as the stuff of literature and its accurate portrayal as a task of serious literary intent. As Eggleston stated the matter in the preface to *The Hoosier Schoolmaster,* "It used to be a matter of no little jealousy with us, I remember, that the manners, customs, thoughts and feelings of New England country people filled so large a place in books, while our life, not less interesting, not less romantic, and certainly not less filled with humorous and grotesque material, had no place in literature." [2] The emphasis on "humorous and grotesque material" should be particularly noted.

The regional movement in the East and South produced novelists and story writers more concerned about delineating the paradisal aspects of life in small towns and rural communities. Sarah Orne Jewett's *Deephaven* (1877) was the first of a series of collections of stories depicting the richness and gentle beauty of life in the small towns and farmhouses of Maine. "People talk about dwelling upon the trivialities and commonplaces in life," she wrote; "but a master writer gives everything weight, and makes you feel the distinction and importance of it."

Mary Murfree's sketches of life in Tennessee poor-white communities, beginning with *In the Tennessee Mountains* (1884), are notable not merely for their evocations of scenic splendors but for their realistic descriptions of courting, gambling, drinking, working, fighting, and general merrymaking among the Tennessee mountain folk. Both Miss Jewett and Miss Murfree have an eye for the idiosyncratic and grotesque in their rural characters, while Miss Murfree, like some other writers of the regional school, sought to produce phonetically accurate transcriptions of the dialect of her characters by means of heavily apostrophized contractions, barbarous misspellings, and the use of local idioms. The celebration of common people and commonplace living is the unifying factor in the work of the provincial realists and local colorists.

In his modern English "Victorian" poems Riley provided a poetic equivalent to the domestic, sentimental, pious romance which had dominated magazine fiction during the period from 1850 to 1870. "An Old Sweetheart of Mine" hits just the right tone. In certain poems ("A Tress of Hair," "The Passing of a Heart," and "In the Corridor" are examples) we may see an equivalent to those situation paintings of tender moments in the lives of upper middle-class young lovers that were another staple item of ladies' magazines and albums of the period, while "Nothin' to Say" and "The Old Man and Jim" are like situation paintings of emotional crises in the lives of humbler people. In yet another group of poems, including "Baby's Dying," "On the Death of Little Mahala Ashcraft," "Give Me the Baby," and "When Bessie Died," we may discern that characteristic Victorian sense of moral uplift—a purification of spirit provided by death, especially that of children— which is found in popular fiction, English and American, in the second half of the nineteenth century. One need look no further that Dickens for examples.

These parallels with popular fiction are borne out in Riley's work in dialect. Like the provincial realists and the local colorists he attempts to render exactly the speech of his small-town types and Hoosier farmers. Like the local colorists, he has a particular eye for the idiosyncratic and eccentric in the characters he describes. He enlarges the nostalgic, sentimental aspect of the humorists, discernible in Twain and Harte, until the fairly wide range of character types he presents—very old and very young, deeply rural and faintly citified, enterprising and stick-in-the-mud —is blended in an overall wash of sentimentality. Though the young may be mischief-loving and the old curmudgeonly, there is almost invariably a sound grounding of good in their characters, while the central figures of the rural narratives are often didactically heroic in the face of adversity.

## III  *The Small Town Scene*

The core of Riley's work and its main interest for the literary historian are found in the idealized picture of Middle Western small-town and rural life which he presents. In *A Child-World*, his most sustained effort at a unified volume, the framework is a genre-picture of an evening's neighborly entertainment in a small-town household, though the bulk of the book is occupied by the narratives which the characters offer for each other's enjoyment. *The Rubaiyat of Doc Sifers* covers a wide range of rural activities, from ditchdigging and harvesting, to cooking, lodge activities, group philosophizing, childrearing, beekeeping, drinking, hunting, fishing, firefighting, circus-going, "cussing," parading, and praying; but these are simply the means of revealing the extraordinary extent of Doc's talents and the abiding goodness of his character. This poem presents the underlying philosophy of small-town life, suitably idealized, in action. The "Johnson of Boone" poems present the same philosophy, touched by the quizzical character of their protagonist, in meditation. The active side of this philosophy expresses a sense of service and goodwill towards one's fellow humans; its passive side a genial enjoyment of the good things of life ( good weather, good food, good company, and the chance to be lazy), overlying a nostalgic, even melancholy, awareness of the passing of earthly joys.

In those volumes which collect the shorter pieces, Riley creates, in poem after poem, the characters and properties which form a broad picture of small-town life conceived in ideal terms. We hear little of its discomforts and its limitations, apart from those disputes and rivalries which make life go. Its people, its institutions, and its commonplace material trappings are there to be enjoyed; and the limitation ( as the poems contrasting city with small-town life imply) enhances the enjoyment.

For characters, a number of farmers, cautious and hardworking, philosophical and enduring, have already been encountered in the discussion of the rural narratives and the "Johnson of Boone" poems. Hired hands and hired girls (and *our* hired man, "The Raggedy Man," and *our* hired girl) appear in some of the narratives and in a number of individual poems. Young beaux and belles of varying degrees of reliability and flightiness people the rural narratives. Not infrequently their courting is linked with the conduct of some small-town activity. "Christmas along the Wires" is narrated in the telegraph office of the Hoosier Railroad Station, Washout Glen. Its subject is the courtship by MacClintock (telegraph operator of ". . . this little eight-by-ten/Dinky town of Washout Glen") of Brownie, beautiful sixteen-year-old operator at Pilot Knob (and, like Armazindy, a heroic fatherless child), and of MacClintock's rivalry with "Roachy," the smoother operator at the slightly less small town of Roachdale. The whole action of the narrative, which builds to a climax at a Christmas dance, hinges on the importance of the telegraph as a link enabling the safe running of the railroad between the three communities.

In "At 'The Literary'," another yarn of courtship, the narrator's courtship of Izory is brought to a successful conclusion by his understanding of the importance of the settlement's Literary Society in attaining social distinction. The narrator is at first reluctant to join; he finds social pleasures enough:

> Us folks in the country sees
> *Lots* o' fun!—Take spellin' school;
> Er ole hoe-down jamborees;
> Er revivals; er ef you'll
> Tackle taffy-pullin's you
> Kin git fun, and quite a few!—
> Same with huskin's.

Compared with this catalogue of social pleasures, the Literary Society seems redundant:

> First they started it—" 'y gee!"
> Thinks-says-I "this settle-ment
> 'S gittin' too high-toned fer me!"

But, when all began to join, he "jest kind o' drapped in line" and is appointed "Critic" on the very first night. After a debate on "Which air more destructive element, fire er worter" and some singing, the essay competition begins. By pronouncing Izory's piece the "Best thing in the whole concern," the "Critic" manages for the first time to reach an understanding with her.

A number of poems point up the importance in settlement life of Christmas festivities, which become a favorite scene for the announcement of a successful courtship (courting in Riley is invariably proper, though it may be conducted in secret), or, in the "sad" poems, provide an ironic backdrop to some scene of domestic tragedy.

"Goin' to the Fair" and "In Fervent Praise of Picnics" present a child's-eye view of two of the longed-for occasional pleasures of small-town life, and incidental allusions to the fun of the fair abound in other poems. "Fire at Night" is a graphic little picture of another occasional source of excitement for young and old.

"Bin a-Fishin'," "The Fishin' Party," and a number of other poems, the best of them perhaps "Up and Down Old Brandy-wine," express the unfailing pleasures of this form of rural recreation. The mood here is generally that of "Knee-Deep in June" or "At Utter Loaf," a kind of philosophical lassitude, a sense of the prodigality of nature and the generosity with which she offers herself. With few exceptions ("The Fishin' Party" is one), fishing brings no frustrations.

A few poems ("A Sudden Shower," "A Canary at the Farm," "Two Sonnets to the June Bug," and "The First Bluebird," for examples) are vignettes of some of the momentary or minor sources of delight to be found in rural living. Others—"Out to Old Aunt Mary's" is the best-known—provide a series of vignettes of the delights to be found in the garden, about the house, or in "far fields, bottom-lands, creek-banks." "The Old Swimmin'-Hole" celebrates another unfailing source of enjoyment for the small-town or village boy.

In "The Old Band" a farmer, returned after twenty years in Kansas, contrasts the virtues of the "old band" with the new, reminisces about the musicians he knew and the tunes they played, and records in the process the importance of this small-town institution in the life he has known.

Some poems are written in praise of the familiar objects of rural life. "The Old Trundle-Bed" has been discussed in a previous chapter. "The Old Family Bible" is a solemn example; "The Old Hay-Mow," "My Fiddle," and "Uncle William's Picture" are light-hearted.

## IV  *Characters*

Riley is not generally thought of as a creator of character. There is no single character, like Hay's Jim Bledsoe or Harte's Jack Hamlin, who springs to mind when his name is mentioned. Yet it is possible by judicious selection to assemble from his work a range of small-town and rural types almost as wide as those in Edgar Lee Masters' *Spoon River Anthology,* though Riley's people are certainly not so mordantly observed as these nor possessed by the same social vision.

The characters of Johnson of Boone and Doc Sifers have already been discussed at some length in previous chapters. In the rural narratives and in the shorter poems the characters are in general more lightly sketched in, though there are frequent deft touches of character revelation. The background of these characters is set in "A Tale of the Airly Days," a plea for "Somepin' a pore man understands/With his feelin's's well as ears," which will not dress up the truth:

> Tell me a tale of the timber lands
>   Of the old-time pioneers;
> .    .    .    .    .    .    .    .
> Say they was 'leven in the fambily—
>   Two beds, and the chist, below,
> And the trundle-beds that each helt three,
>   And the clock and the old bureau.

But although in the narratives and poems, privations, difficulties, and the hard facts of experience abound, there is much dressing up of the truth of character. Though meanness and hardness of character are to be expected in a limited society, they are not much in evidence in Riley's characters. In general, the means of revelation of character in the narratives are the trials of love (between courting couples or in the family) and of farming. In the shorter poems brief character sketches are the rule, but in some cases the resulting figures are more fully rounded than the character who is revealed in action in the narratives.

As an example, we may compare a narrative, admittedly brief, like "A New Year's Time at Willards's" with a poem like "Coon-

Dog Wess." In the former, the courtship of the hired man, Tomps McClure for S'repty Willards, the farmer's daughter, brings out the character of farmer Willards when he hears that McClure

> . . . tuk
> A shine to S'repty Willards.—Then
> You'd ort'o see the old man buck
> An' hist hisse'f an' paw the dirt,
>     An' hint that "common workin'-men
>     That didn't want their feelin's hurt
> 'Ud better hunt fer 'compn'y' where
> The folks was pore an' didn't care!"

But the details of the little domestic drama, the gift-giving, a New Year's dinner with the hired hands in the company, and the eventual foiling of farmer Willards by the connivance of his other daughter Marg'et do not reveal much of the way of life or of the social attitudes of the characters.

"Coon-Dog Wess" is the tale of a coon-hunter who "moved in this-here Settlement" from the next county in the spring of 1867. The comic touches, as Wess appears with " 'long 'bout forty-'leven orneriest-lookin' hounds" and his wife "traipsin' at the rag-tag-and-bobtail of the crowd, dogs and childern," and the sentimental touches concerning his wife's devotion to him after he is lamed in felling a tree—these are the expected trappings of a Riley yarn; but we feel at the end of the poem that we have understood something of the life of the settlement in the descriptions of the neighbors' tolerance and help for Wess in spite of the noise of his hounds and the haphazard, work-shy mode of his existence.

Other poems present briefer pictures of small-town and rural types. "My Fiddle" offers a sketch of the country fiddler, a necessary part of every small-town dance. "The Country Editor" is a brief plea for mercy for this necessary but much maligned small-town figure. "Herr Weiser"—"Transplanted here in the Hoosier loam,/And blossomy as his German home"—is a rather sentimental tribute to the immigrant farmer. Preachers do not often appear in Riley's poems, though Daddy Barker in the prose "An Old Settler's Story" is a full portrait. The deacon of "Sister Jones's Confession" is a background figure. "The Preacher's Boy," a yarn about the ne'er-do-well son of a holy man, hints at Riley's preference for

goodness expressed in courageous action rather than the uttered
goodness of approved religion.

A favorite Riley character is the coward or weakling who turns
up trumps in the end, preferably in some courageous act that
brings about his death. "This Man Jones" is one such:

> A feller 'at had no sand at all;
> Kind o' consumpted, and undersize,
> And sallor-complected, with big sad eyes
> And a kind-of-a-sort-of-a hang-dog style,
> And a sneakin' sort-of-a half-way smile
> 'At kind o' give him away to us
> As a preacher, maybe, er somepin' wuss.

The revelation of group social attitudes and preferences in this
passage is very notable. Jones achieves a somewhat comic heroic
death saving the "Lion Queen" of a circus from an angry lion.

"Joney," no connection apparently, is a harelipped boy, the constant butt of jeers from the boys and of cruel indifference from the
girls (another revelation of social attitudes); but he meets a heroic end in saving thirteen children in a drowning accident. His
body, found three days later, is identified only by his mouth.
"Scotty" has been discussed earlier, the tale of a ne'er-do-well boy
who dies a hero in the Civil War. "Tom Johnson's Quit" is a clever
variation on the temperance poem and another sly revelation of
social attitudes. In discussing the subject of temperance, "a passel
o' the boys" refuses to believe the sudden news that Tom Johnson,
the town drunk, has quit, until it is further revealed that he has
staggered in front of "the Ten Express"; the refrain which provides the title has now an ironic sting.

"Jap Miller" and "John McKeen" are contrasting portraits of
two rural politicians. The first, unchanged by power, is untiring in
his defense of the common-man's rights and always one of the
people—"There's where the feller's stren'th lays,—he's so common-
like and plain." John McKeen, on the other hand, has "grown ambitious in worldly ways," abandoned the interests and the style of
life of the people who elected him to office, and set himself up in
a mansion, with his wife a recluse and his daughters at finishing
school. The types are stereotypes, but the emphasis on a "common-
like and plain" style of living is important.

Riley's portraits of farmers have already been sufficiently noted, but his sketches of farmer's wives and the women of small towns deserve attention. The favorite female character of a Riley story is the heroically enduring woman, working untiringly to hold the family together, such a type as "Evagene Baker, Who Was Dyin' of Dred Consumption as These Lines Was Penned by a True Friend"—the mock heroic frame here recalls the "Johnson of Boone" poems. The verdict on Evagene is that she doesn't need praying for; all she needed was "more playin'." Another frequent character is the simple-hearted lass, steadfastly loving. "Marthy Ellen," who elopes with her man in spite of the constant opposition of both their families, is one of many examples.

Riley's female characters are in general more idealized and less differentiated than his male characters, but he presents the other side occasionally in such figures as the husband-hungry Sister Jones and the termagant or untenderhearted wives of "Mylo Jones's Wife" or "My First Womern."

Although this enumeration of some of the figures from Riley's poems may demonstrate that his characterization is fairly wide in social function and status, within the limited milieu he chose to describe, it could not be claimed that Riley is a great creator of character. We might say that he creates a fully rounded character, in that he has produced a recognizable human type, with some account of defects and merits. To some of the admiring critics of Riley's own time, even to such a doubting admirer as Hamlin Garland, he had hit the characteristics of the Hoosier farmer to the life. Yet none of his characters has achieved independent existence; they are not, in any sense of the term, literary immortals.

The Hoosier of "Like His Mother Used to Make," returning to his home state after twenty years away, finds himself instantly at home. The unifying quality of almost all Riley's characters is that they belong. They are firmly rooted in the small town and rural world of Riley's creation; they accept its limitations ungrudgingly and proudly reject the claims of superiority of a citified or "elegant" world. Almost uniquely in American poetry, for Whitman does not create "characters" in this sense, they are totally unalienated from their world, which is of course a real world only at several removes. There could be no greater contrast with the characters of Riley's successor in the poetic depiction of Middle

Western small-town life, those of Edgar Lee Masters in the *Spoon River Anthology*.

### V  *Humor*

If Riley is not a great creator of character, wherein does his humor lie? Much of it is purely verbal. When, in his "Lines to Perfesser John Clark Ridpath," Riley recalls for the farm boy become scholar that he "baked [his] face/A-readin' Plutark Slives all night by that old fi-er place," the poet is following in the well-worn path of comic rustic ignorance pioneered by Petroleum V. Nasby and Artemus Ward. The crudely humble metaphors of the narrator of "At 'The Literary'," who describes how, after all the settlement have joined,

> I jest kind o' drapped in line,
> Like you've seen some sandy, thin,
> Scrawny shoat putt fer the crick
> Down some pig-trail through the thick
> Spice-bresh, where the whole drove's been
> 'Bout six weeks 'fore he gits in!

—such metaphors as these, and examples abound, are part of the rambling style that was the stock-in-trade of the nineteenth-century American humorists from Seba Smith to Twain.

The droll turn of phrase is another quality Riley shares with these humorists, like Twain's description of the jack rabbit— "Long after he is out of sight, you can hear him whiz." Riley does not do it so well, but here is an example from "Armazindy," who was orphaned when

> Her father blowed
> Up—eternally furloughed—
> When the old "Sultana" bu'st,
> And sich men wuz needed wusst.

None of these qualities alone, however, even when joined to Riley's undoubted metrical skill and ability to create lively dialogue in dialect verse, is sufficient to account for his immense popularity as a writer of humorous verse about Hoosier small-town and farm life.

Riley's greatest comic creation is an outlook, an attitude to life, as expressed in the implied character of the narrator or narrators of the dialect poems. Viewed in a derogatory light, this attitude to life resembles Bernard de Voto's appraisal of Sinclair Lewis: "He had the mind of a cheer leader. Ploughboy gaping at the eternal dawn. Diurnal wonder of the tremendous platitude. Periodical discovery of the utterly apparent." [3] But the Hoosier farmer of the "Johnson of Boone" poems, quizzical, ignorant, musing, occasionally melancholy, yet humbly grateful for a good life, and the simple souls of the rural narratives, cheerfully pursuing their simple joys or facing their daunting adversities, represented for the many thousands who bought Riley's books and read them again and again a quixotic faith in human nature and the simple strength of its grass roots.

This affirmation of faith does not alone account for Riley's great popularity, much of which derived from his sentimental verse and the wistful nostalgia of his depiction of Middle Western life. But, if we are to look for the source of his appeal as a humorous writer, it is in this context that it must be understood. In spite of superficial similarities, Riley's humor is in many respects aside from the mainstream of American literary humor in the nineteenth century. It eschews social satire almost entirely, and it substitutes an expansive geniality for the shrewdness and wit of his predecessors.

CHAPTER *9*

# Significant Popularity

THE rapid decline in Riley's reputation that followed his death in 1916 is not likely to be reversed. The chief obstacle to enthusiasm facing any reader today who reads him at length is the sheer badness of much of his work. Whole stanzas and whole poems, by the dozen, particularly among the Victorian-style poems, are remarkable for their flatulence of diction and shoddy construction. The frequently inept phrasing, the plunges into bathos, the lapses of taste in the modern English poems, the limp irresolution of conclusions, the tiresome repetition of particular sentiments in poem after poem, the absence of any psychological depth or realism in characterization, the irritating narrowness of outlook inevitable in the chosen milieu—all these characteristics militate against the enjoyment of his work by a reader of the present day.

Riley's fame as a children's writer also appears to be on the decline, although he is still anthologized in collections for children. A biography on his life was included in Bobbs-Merrill's "Childhood of Famous Americans" series as recently as 1942, and the copyright was renewed in 1962. But, as far as my limited personal knowledge goes, the "Raggedy Man" poems and even "Little Orphant Annie" do not produce any instant response in the American schoolchild today. The dialect and the wandering narrative line of the longer children's poems also present special difficulties. Only the brief poems for the very young, pieces like "Extremes," seem to have retained their freshness untarnished.

Even in his own day, Riley's work was not highly rated by most of the few academic critics then writing, and the limited acknowledgment accorded by E. C. Stedman, in his *An American Anthology* (1900) was felt as a signal honor. A few Riley poems are included in the first *Oxford Book of American Verse* (1927), but this collection was edited by Bliss Carman, an admirer and occasional imitator of Riley and not an academic critic. We do not find or expect to find any poem by Riley in the later *Oxford Book of American Verse* (1950), edited by F. O. Matthiessen.

The inclusion of a very modest piece by Riley, "Goodby er Howdy Do," in Ezra Pound's idiosyncratic but valuable anthology, *Confucius to Cummings* (1964), may suggest that the emerging poets of the first decade of the twentieth century found some value in Riley's natural handling of speech rhythms and general simplicity of outlook in a barren period of American poetry, marked by pretentiousness of language and subject. We may recall Kipling's praise in a letter to Riley in 1893. Kipling pays warm tribute to the genuineness of Riley's work against "the precious, self-conscious get-on-my-curves stuff that is solemnly put forward as the great American exhibit!" [1]

The traveller in southern Indiana discovers that Riley's regional fame endures, but it is also apparent that his depiction of the Hoosier type as a representation of the American common man becomes increasingly remote and increasingly unflattering to regional pride.

In the last years of his life Riley received many honors and marks of recognition from his home state, from the national government, and from academic institutions. These, we may feel today, were a recognition not of the intrinsic merit of his work but of the universal acclamation it had been accorded by the general populace and of the fame of Riley as a beloved personality. Though the extent of Riley's writing, touring, and reciting sharply declined in the last fifteen years of his life, he became in these years almost a symbolic figure, the living repository of the cherished values of simplicity, honesty, and unsophistication in a society which in many respects had moved away from these values.

## I  *Reasons for Popularity*

The most popular of Riley's poems were among his worst. "An Old Sweetheart of Mine" and "Out to Old Aunt Mary's" were enormously popular as platform items and in illustrated editions, and they long retained their popularity as recitation pieces. But as poetry they are notably bad. "Little Orphant Annie," also an outstanding popular and commercial success, is a good children's poem, but it is not great or even very good poetry. We may attribute the success of these individual pieces to the generally low standard of public taste in poetry, but this does not account for the general public adoption of Riley as a personality and of the milieu of his Hoosier poems as a true representation of the American way of life.

It is perhaps in the widespread popularity of Riley's work and in the general acceptance of his depiction of Middle Western life that Riley's true significance for the literary historian lies. The idealized version of life presented by Riley made that life more acceptable for his age by romanticizing it, for the ugliness of reality is escaped if it is sweetened and softened. On the other hand, if the version presented was "wholesome to the core," it would serve to reaffirm and strengthen the qualities needed to endure in an age of rapid and sweeping material and social growth and change. The rapidity of growth is reflected in the changes of population in the last decades of the nineteenth century. "In the decade after the war," the historians Charles and Mary Beard record, "nearly seven million persons were added to the population of the country. . . . By 1870, the population of the United States had risen to 38,500,000; by 1880, 50,100,000; by 1900, to 76,100,000."

This was also a period of new inventions "on which new industries of gigantic proportions were constructed"; of phenomenal growth of railroad mileage, so that "countless little towns and villages in far-scattered rural regions were linked to the great cities and with one another"; and also a period of which it could be said that "in the history of political corruption, seldom, if ever, had there been transactions on a scale so prodigious or conducted with more brazen effrontery." [2] If times were dull, they were fraught with change and with peril.

In common with many previous periods of human history, the full social consequences of material change lagged behind, and it was not until the period following World War I that they were fully implemented. The Gilded Age "was one of rapid change, of the introduction of much that was new and disturbing in American life; traditional values were severely tested, some of them not surviving and others surviving only in modified form." [3] The "repetition of given facts" and the reaffirmation of traditional values were needed as a stabilizing element. It is the role of popular culture to supply these qualities. or was until comparatively recent times; and they are especially notable in the popular culture of the Gilded Age.

It was the quality of reaffirmation, of reassurance, which made Riley's work of significance and value to his own age. As Alfred Kreymborg noted, Riley "served an ideal curiously akin to Whitman's." [4] If we are tempted to regard this as a manifestation of the inevitable tendency of popular culture to debase the styles and the fundamental myths of "élite" art to the level of genre and cliché, it could, of course, be pointed out that Whitman wrote for a popular audience, was a newspaper writer, and was not fully acclimated into élite and academic levels until many years after his death.

As we have noted elsewhere, it was a popular pastime among newspaper critics of the first two decades of the twentieth century to debate the reasons for Riley's popularity and in the years after his death to discuss the question whether he was a national poet. A columnist in the New York *Evening Post* stated the derogatory side of the commonly accepted reason for his popularity: "Your Hoosier, when he is waxed fat, when his bank account and limousine give assurance of a comfort and a luxury to which his boyhood was a stranger, does not forget those old, but happy far-off days. . . . Not, be it understood, that he would go back there if he could. But Riley sings of that longing for the simple life which we all deceive ourselves occasionally into thinking we feel." [5]

The best statement of the case for Riley as a national poet is contained in Henry A. Beers' essay "The Singer of the Old Swimmin' Hole," collected in his *The Connecticut Wits and Other Essays* in 1920. For Beers, who was a Professor of English at Yale, Riley was a national poet, greater than Whitman. "As to any dramatic power to discriminate among individuals and characterize them singly, as Riley does," Beers asserts, "Whitman had none. They are all alike, all 'leaves of grass'. . . . We do not thrill to Walt Whitman's paeans to democracy in the abstract; but we vibrate to every cord on the theme of family affections, of early friendships, and of the dear old homely things that our childhood knew. Americans are sentimental and humorous; and Riley abounds in sentiment—wholesome sentiment—and natural humor, while Whitman had little of either." [6]

The tribute of Beers, whose tastes were formed in the closing years of the nineteenth century, was in fact the swan song of critical acclamation. By 1938, Richard A. Cordell's summary judgment in the *Saturday Review* was the typical one:

> James Whitcomb Riley reports the uneducated Hoosier's bad grammar rather than his dialect, and he idealizes country life—Riley never lived on a farm and, unlike Hamlin Garland, had no experience with its back-breaking toil.[7] He will always be remembered for a few pieces like "Little Orphant Annie" and "The Raggedy Man," which have passed into folklore, but it is unlikely that school children in Glasgow and Dumfries will ever read Riley (with glossary) as children in Indianapolis and Greenfield read Burns.[8]

## II  *The Idea of the Small Town*

The overall quality, or lack of quality of Riley's work, does not lead us to expect any significant "legacy of influence." In terms of popular newspaper verse, we may discern his influence as a purveyor of homely wisdom at work in the prosaic soothsaying of Edgar Guest and others who are of no significance in the annals of literature.

Any attempt to suggest an influence from popular verse such as Riley's on the work of any poet of importance in American literary history must be fraught with peril. Yet it is perhaps permissible to note in passing a comment by Leon Edel, in reviewing the collected letters of Robert Frost: "[Frost's] most winning mask is that of the contrived rustic, the rural curmudgeon, offering the wisdom of the soil." [9]

The wide geographical and social range of Riley's popularity by the first decade of the twentieth century is attested by the mounting crescendo of tributes accorded him in the period from 1902 to his death in 1916. He had by these years become a part of the national consciousness, and the idealized version of rural and small-town life which he presented became a pervasive idea, a counterpoise to the idea of the big city which was to become increasingly significant as the century advanced. If we are to look for Riley's "influence" in the writers of the generation after his, we should look not for verbal parallels or wholesale borrowings but for the continuing development, the rejection or adaptation of the idea of the small town as demiparadise, of which he was the great progenitor and arch popularizer.

The lines of this development are traced in great detail by Ima Herron in *The Small Town in American Literature*. It may suffice here to state that the chief agent for this development was Booth Tarkington, a native of Indianapolis who had known Riley from his early teens and became a lifelong friend. Of greater significance, however, was the reaction against the semiparadisal (or phony) version of rural and small-town life by Edgar Lee Masters in poetry and by Sinclair Lewis in the novel. Their "realism" was itself limited by comparison with the social realism of Dreiser (whose work, incidentally, Riley disliked almost as much as he disliked that of Whitman) or of James T. Farrell. Part of the irritated rejection of the Rileyan idealized picture of rural and small-town life by the generation of Masters and Lewis stemmed from the fact that this idealism was frequently masqueraded as realism. Riley's introduction to a public reading in Chicago in October, 1900, illustrates this dubious notion of realism. It was his usual style of introduction:

> I have to offer this evening some homely specimens, with your kindly tolerance, of the dialect that is peculiar to our Western American country, and these specimens, I may say, are intended to be conscientious studies of the people and their peculiar feelings and characteristics, as well as of their home language, which is their native tongue. I do not know how better to begin, because I want to gain your favor by relieving you of any possible fear that I am going to administer a lecture, and therefore I will at once offer you a character sketch of an old country farmer, seventy years of age, the pioneer American type . . . we must remember . . . that this splendid type of the old man goes hand-in-hand with the all-kind Mother Nature, lives in the green fields and near the still waters, where the opportunity for contemplation is near the heart of Nature.[10]

The reality presented is a highly selective, softened, idealized reality, but a genuine one within its own limitations and genuinely representative of a particular regional outlook on life. Both Masters and Sinclair Lewis appreciated and responded to this aspect of the Rileyan view of life. As an undergraduate at Yale, Lewis wrote a typically enthusiastic panegyric on Riley for the *Yale Literary Magazine*. His editorial is worth quoting in full, as evidence of his familiarity with Riley's work:

> To make a book joyaunce, Fitzgerald uses the Persian rose, its damask petals heavy with age-old wine. The French prefer frank sensualism. As Arthur Stirling said, "They are full of the Gallic disease." Whittier fancied more the morning light which glittered on the armour of Launcelot, without the sodden heart therein. His was practically a Yale attitude. James Whitcomb Riley, with a lyric lilt and melody denied the Quaker, makes as primary an appeal to Americans; and his "Benj. Johnson" is as clear-eyed and pregnantly optimistic as "Hosea Bigelow." One Giuseppe Rochietti wrote, "Why a National Literature Cannot Flourish in the United States." His question is a favorite one with many academicians, who babble of heterogeneity and the lack of American legendry, while Riley is making the said literature.
>
> The golden haze of poetry is a magnifying medium. We must have "seers," if we shall learn rightly to adore Achates, or the sky lark, or Dan Paine. A forgotten bard has implored
>
> > "As Provence gleameth, most revealed
> > In little lyrics of the field,
> > So shine our Western land."
>
> And Boyland! There awaits us, under the sick-a-more, Hamey and Bud. The Raggedy Man whittles there, with an Utopian jack-knife, while we yearn for our return from the realm of sophistication and wrinkled *ennui,* that his tales may set our narrowed lips laughing, our slow hearts rippling. Alice of Wonderland, and Orphant Annie, and the spirit of Hovey[11] will give us a place in the circle which listens to Benj.'s fiddle, with its "Kink o' drivin' care away." There is a wonderful secret in this land of Romaunts, one for which Ponce de Leon went questing. A Pied Piper it is, whose pictures entice us to his innocent Venusberg. You long for that Phoenix, a friend? He paints our Old Sweethearts, and Billy Miller, who will lead us again to the haunts of l'Allegro. Yes, and of Il Penseroso, as he "philosophizes" in the hay-mow! Oh to be at Utter Loaf, to "Feel through every happy line the tonic of the Spring"; to be *content.* Pied Piper, yours is a siren note! [12]

Masters, twelve years after the publication of *Spoon River Anthology,* wrote a long and appreciative appraisal of Riley's work which recognizes the limitations and values the virtues. This brief quotation conveys the gist and tone of his appraisal:

> Indiana was a happy Country Fair to [Riley], which he saw under unusual advantages, and with eyes peculiarly gifted for gathering in what was quaint and joyous and innocent in country and village life. . . . Riley did not wish, even if he could have done so, to go behind the happy appearances of the Fair. He might mention at times that there were fights, that some one was "stobbed"; but he did not penetrate to dramatic reasons. The old fiddler was always lovable, never trivial or clownish. The pioneers were heroic figures of the land-clearing days, of the trials of the wilderness, of the log-cabin with its happy simplicities. If they were prudent and sagacious old land traders who made good use of their chances, that was not for poetical treatment. He showed the Fair and its personages in their holiday dress, gay and amiable, laughing and feasting; if grieving or wounded, tenderly attended, and if ludicrous, still lovable.[13]

But, although Riley was there to be enjoyed, his version of the truth would not do. "It is not too much to say," according to Jennette Tandy, "that the whole of *Spoon River Anthology* is an arraignment of the hypocrisy and the futility of the conventional morality preached by the unlettered philosopher." [14] As Ima Herron notes, Masters is "interested in the ironic contrast between *what is believed* and *what is true* about the Spoon River villagers." [15] The facts of hypocrisy, meanness, greed, lust, and materialism are revealed beneath respectable exteriors, or the fact of relative honesty is sometimes revealed beneath a disreputable exterior. Yet even this post-mortem dissection of the truth of small-town life does not exclude those who are lifted to a plane of exaltation and who express the idealism and exuberance which are the basic qualities of Riley's presentation.

In his monumental biography of Sinclair Lewis, Mark Schorer makes no mention of James Whitcomb Riley; but there is some evidence to suggest that it was in part at least the Rileyan presentation of small-town life, once enthusiastically endorsed, against which Lewis was reacting in *Main Street,* if we may accept Carol Kennicott's discovery of the truth about Middle Western small-town life as a faithful reflection of Lewis's views:

In reading popular stories and seeing plays, asserted Carol, she had found only two traditions of the American small town. The first tradition, repeated in scores of magazines every month, is that the American village remains the one sure abode of friendship, honesty, and clean, sweet marriageable girls. . . . The other tradition is that the significant features of all villages are whiskers, iron dogs upon lawns, gold bricks, checkers, jars of gilded cattails and shrewd comic old men who are known as "hicks" and who ejaculate "Waal I swan."

The two traditions, Carol finds, are in fact one, and both are opposed to the reality, which

is an unimaginatively standardized background, a sluggishness of speech and manners, a rigid ruling of the spirit by the desire to appear respectable. It is . . . the contentment of the quiet dead, who are scornful of the living for their restless walking. It is negation canonized as the one positive virtue. It is the prohibition of happiness. It is slavery self-sought and self-defended. It is dullness made God.[16]

In the brilliant scene describing a social evening at Gopher Prairie in Chapter IV of *Main Street*, Carol hears Miss Ella Stowbody, "the spinster daughter of the Ionic bank . . . our shark at elocuting," recite "An Old Sweetheart of Mine"; and she is to hear it nine times more during the ensuing winter.

If the culture of Gopher Prairie is a spurious one, it is the product of a desire not unlike Carol's to impose the higher culture on the crude life of Gopher Prairie. As Carol further discovers, the higher culture is not without its perils; dullness as a fact cannot be erased, and it may itself conceal virtues which are heroic and of enduring value.

The significance of James Whitcomb Riley as the creator of an effective stereotype of American small-town life which enjoyed widespread popular acceptance had been perhaps unduly overlooked by literary historians. It produced no successors of importance, but a significant reaction. The idea of the small town as demiparadise had meaning for his contemporaries, but it has lost its value as a significant focus in the literary interpretation of American life. The last work of any note to exploit it was Thornton Wilder's *Our Town* (1938).

Yet, while it is not possible to claim any especial intrinsic merit for any of Riley's poems, it is still possible for the reader today to enjoy a few of them as period pieces; and they do occasionally amuse as the nineteenth-century prose humorists, apart from Twain and Harte, rarely do. There is, of course, a perverse pleasure to be derived from the reading of bad verse, as the devotees of William MacGonagall, bad poet of Dundee, have discovered; and there is pleasure of this type in plenty in reading Riley's Victorian-style poems. The reader in quest of a more honest enjoyment of humorous light verse would be advised to restrict his attentions to Riley's dialect poems. The rural narratives, when due allowance is made for the stock nature of the sentiments, can still entertain by the liveliness of their use of dialogue; and the shorter poems, such pieces as "A Summer's Day" or "A Pen-Pictur' of a Cert'in Frivvolus Old Man," judiciously selected, have retained an authentic period charm.

# Notes and References

## Chapter One

1. Lewis Leary, *John Greenleaf Whittier* (New York, 1961), 80.
2. Hamlin Garland, *Roadside Meetings* (New York, 1930), 225.
3. Richard Crowder, *Those Innocent Years* (Indianapolis, 1957), 208.
4. Roy Harvey Pearce, *The Continuity of American Poetry* (Princeton, 1961), 233.
5. Marcus Dickey, *The Maturity of James Whitcomb Riley* (Indianapolis, 1922), 179; hereafter cited as *Maturity*.
6. *The Letters of James Whitcomb Riley*, ed. William Lyon Phelps (Indianapolis, 1930), 37; letter to G. C. Hitt, January 3, 1882. Hereafter cited as *Letters*.
7. Frank Luther Mott, *A History of American Magazines*, 1885–1905 (Cambridge, Mass., 1957), 43.
8. Dickey, *Maturity*, 221.
9. Pearce, *op. cit.*, 193.
10. *Harper's Magazine* (May, 1891), 965.
11. Quoted in Dickey, *Maturity*, 284.
12. *Ibid.*, 389.
13. *Ibid.*, 409.
14. See, e.g., *Letters*, 183. Letter to Rudyard Kipling, March 4, 1893: "The one evident lack or defect of our whole art guild. . . . It's *business*. . . . So I've gone to work to change that status of affairs. In consequence I'm a revelation to myself. Am making not only 'oodles' of money off my books but twice over as much again by personally reading the same to packed houses." See also "Literature as Business," *Literary History of the United States* (New York, 1948), II, 953–68.
15. R. W. B. Lewis, *The American Adam* (Chicago, 1955), 3.

## Chapter Two

1. Mark Schorer, *Sinclair Lewis; An American Life* (New York, 1961), 4.

2. The creek near which Greenfield was built.

3. Marcus Dickey, *The Youth of James Whitcomb Riley* (Indianapolis, 1919), 14–15; hereafter cited as *Youth*.

4. Matthew Arnold, *Civilization in the United States* (Boston, 1888), 96.

5. James Whitcomb Riley claimed to be of Irish origin, and his Irishness was a part of his public personality. In fact, his grandfather, Andrew Riley (who sometimes spelled the name Riland) was born in Pennsylvania into a Pennsylvania Dutch family which claimed descent from Paulus Reylandt, who had come to Pennsylvania from Holland in 1750. Riley's mother, born Elizabeth Marine, was a second generation American. Her grandfather was born in Wales and was presumably of Huguenot descent. See Crowder, *op. cit.*, p. 13. On Riley's claim to Irish descent see Dickey, *Youth*, 255.

6. Arnold, *op. cit.*, 71.

7. *The Complete Works of James Whitcomb Riley*, ed. Edmund H. Eitel (Indianapolis, 1913), VI, 294–310. The Biographical edition, hereafter cited as *Biog.* Unless otherwise stated, all quotations of Riley's verse and prose are from this edition. I have not in general provided page references to verse quotations since most of the poems are relatively short and the edition is fully indexed.

8. Schorer, *op. cit.*, 144–49.

9. Dickey, *Youth*, 331 ff.

10. Not collected. See Dickey, *Youth*, 339.

11. "Willie," later titled "Prior to Miss Belle's Appearance," *Biog.*, I, 175.

12. Dickey, *Youth*, 383.

13. Letter to John M. Anderson, Oct. 25, 1877. *Letters*, 16.

14. *Letters*, 15.

15. *Love Letters of . . . James Whitcomb Riley to Miss Elizabeth Kahle*, (Boston, 1922), 106, 113, 134.

16. Dickey, *Maturity*, 18.

17. *Ibid.*, 80.

18. See John P. Long, "Matthew Arnold Visits Chicago," *University of Toronto Quarterly*, XXIV (1954), 34–45.

19. Richard Hofstadter, *Anti-Intellectualism in American Life* (New York, 1963), 404.

20. Jay Leyda, *The Melville Log* (New York, 1951), II, 604.

21. Dickey, *Maturity*, 175.

22. See *Publisher's Weekly* (November 26, 1949, and October 14, 1944) on Riley's publishing history and relations with the Bobbs-Merrill Company. See also A. J. and D. R. Russo, *A Bibliography of James Whitcomb Riley* (Indianapolis, 1944).

23. Albert Bigelow Paine, *Mark Twain, A Biography* (New York, 1912), II, 877.

24. *Letters*, 144.

### Chapter Three

1. Dickey, *Maturity*, 214.

2. E.g. "Where Is Mary Alice Smith?" *Biog.*, VI, 272, which describes an orphan girl's stay with a small-town family and was the incident from Riley's childhood which led to the writing of the poem "Little Orphant Annie."

3. Edward Eggleston, *The Hoosier Schoolmaster* (New York, 1871), 5.

4. *Ibid.*, 12.

5. Ima H. Herron, *The Small Town in American Literature* (New York, 1959), 205.

6. *Biog.*, VI, 74.

7. *Ibid.*, VI, 1, 256.

8. George W. Peck's humorous sketches appeared in his own paper, the *Sun*, through the 1870's and were collected in *Peck's Bad Boy and his Pa* (1883).

9. *Biog.*, VI, 245.

10. *Ibid.*, VI, 348. First collected in *Pipes o' Pan at Zekesbury* (Indianapolis, 1888).

11. *Ibid.*, VI, 120. This is the story previously titled "The Boss Girl."

12. Dickey, *Maturity*, 209.

13. *Biog.*, VI, 155.

14. *Ibid.*, VI, 19.

15. The conclusion of "Mrs. Skagg's Husbands." See also, e.g., "The Luck of Roaring Camp," "Tennessee's Partner" and "The Bell-Ringer of Angels."

16. *Letters*, 147.

17. Advertisement at end of 1895 printing.

18. The possible sources of Riley's verse drama might repay further investigation. Perhaps the contemporary literary vogue which provided the idea for Riley's play was the type of children's fairy play represented by William Allingham's *In Fairyland* (1870). Plays of this type are, in general, far less elaborate productions than Riley's is.

19. Cf., for example, Poe's "Fairy-land."

20. The archetypes are the airy and earthy spirits, Ariel and Caliban.

21. Dickey, *Youth*, 325.

22. Russo, *op. cit.*, 39.

23. *Ibid.*, 39.

24. *Letters*, 157.

25. *Ibid.*, 208.

## Chapter Four

1. *Ibid.*, 157.

2. *Ibid.*, 26.

3. *Ibid.*, 31.

4. James Russell Lowell, *A Fable for Critics* (London, 1890), p. 93.

5. *Love Letters . . . to E. Kahle*, 132. Letter dated March 15, 1881.

6. Newton Arvin, *Longfellow, His Life and Work* (Boston, 1963). See especially p. 59, on Longfellow's *The Poets and Poetry of Europe*.

7. William T. Coggeshall, *The Poets and Poetry of the West* (Columbus, Ohio, 1860).

8. The three quotations are from Coggeshall, *op. cit.*, pp. 115, 209, 239.

9. Robert P. Roberts, "Gilt, Gingerbread and Realism: The Public and its Taste," *The Gilded Age: A Reappraisal*, ed. H. Wayne Morgan (Syracuse, N. Y., 1963), 169–95.

10. Borrowing the headings of the "Index by Topics" in *Biog.*, VI, 541–83.

11. Alfred Kreymborg, *Our Singing Strength* (New York, 1929), 235.

12. Bliss Carman, ed. *The Oxford Book of American Verse* (New York, 1927), p. 186.

13. The poem was extended in later versions. See Russo, *op. cit.*, 92.

14. Eliza Cook, "The Old Arm Chair," *The Poets and Poetry of the Nineteenth Century*, vol. [VIII] Joanna Baillie to Jean Ingelow, ed. Alfred H. Miles (London, n.d.), p. 280.

15. Dickey, *Youth*, 325.

16. *Letters*, 30. Letter to Mrs. R. E. Jones, December 22, 1880.

17. Quoted in Crowder, *op. cit.*, 197.

18. William Barnes, "I got two vields," *Selected Poems*, ed. Geoffrey Grigson (London, 1950), p. 101.

19. *Ibid.*, "The Happy Days when I wer Young," 107.

20. *Ibid.*, "The New House a-getten Wold," 180.

21. Arvin, *op. cit.*, 328.

22. Pearce, *op. cit.*, 197.

23. Robert Falk, "The Search for Reality: Writers and their Literature," *The Gilded Age: A Reappraisal*, ed. H. Wayne Morgan (Syracuse, N. Y., 1963), pp. 196–220. See p. 208.

24. Kreymborg, *op. cit.*, 232.

### Chapter Five

1. "On a Youthful Portrait of Stevenson."
2. Robert Louis Stevenson, "The Land of Nod," *Works* (London, 1907), XIII, p. 28.
3. Kenneth Grahame, *Cambridge Book of Poetry for Children*, 2nd ed. (London, 1932).

### Chapter Six

1. Crowder, *op. cit.*, 274.
2. Falk, *op. cit.*, 196.
3. Roberts, *op. cit.*, 171.
4. Pearce, *op. cit.*, 233.
5. Wallace Stegner, "Western Record and Romance," *Literary History of the United States*, ed. Robert E. Spiller and others (New York, 1948), II, 871.
6. *Letters*, 69.
7. Dickey, *Maturity*, 222.
8. *Letters*, 178.
9. *Letters*, 84. Letter dated September 1, 1888.
10. Quoted in Meredith Nicholson, *The Hoosiers* (New York, 1915).
11. *Letters*, 150.
12. Hamlin Garland, *Roadside Meetings* (New York, 1930), pp. 90–97.
13. Bret Harte, *Complete Poetical Works* (New York, n.d.), p. 118.
14. John Hay, *Complete Poetical Works* (Boston, 1917), p. 3.
15. Will Carleton, *Farm Ballads, Farm Festivals and Farm Legends* (London, 1891), p. 47.
16. Garland, *op. cit.*, 97.
17. *Ibid.*, 97.
18. Cf. The crippled Tiny Tim's Christmas wish, "God bless us every one," in Dickens' *A Christmas Carol*. This became Riley's favorite way of signing off a letter in his later years. See also Riley's story "Jamesy."
19. *People* (Indianapolis). See Russo, *op. cit.*, 42.

### Chapter Seven

1. Quoted in Dickey, *Maturity*, 165.
2. William Empson, *English Pastoral Poetry* (New York, 1938), p. 4.
3. Cf. Whittier's "Maud Muller" as a variation on this theme.
4. Empson, *op. cit.*, 14.
5. Cf. Huck's self-questionings concerning Jim, or the opening of

Harris's "How Mr. Rabbit Saved His Meat" where "the little boy" picks up Uncle Remus on a point.

6. Jennette Tandy, *Crackerbox Philosophers in American Humor and Satire* (New York, 1925), p. ix.

7. James Russell Lowell, *Complete Poetical Works* (Cambridge, Mass., n.d.). The "Cambridge Edition." Quotations are from pp. 182, 184, 192, 204.

8. *Biog.*, VI, 378–81.

9. *The Complete Essays of Mark Twain,* ed. Charles Neider (New York, 1963), pp. 155–59.

10. Tandy, *op. cit.,* p. 25.

11. Lowell, *op. cit.,* p. 233. 2nd series, no. II.

12. James Whitcomb Riley and Bill Nye, *Nye and Riley's Wit and Humor* (Chicago, 1905), p. 180. This is a later version of *Nye and Riley's Railway Guide* (Chicago, 1888).

13. Riley and Nye, *op. cit.,* 187.

14. Dickey, *Youth,* 143.

15. Not included in later collected editions.

16. Radcliffe Squires, *The Major Themes of Robert Frost* (Ann Arbor, 1963), p. 56.

17. Quoted in Dickey, *Maturity,* 148.

18. Cf. Leary, *op. cit.,* 144: "in even the simplest of [Whittier's] pastoral poems the attitudes are cultivated."

19. John B. Pickard, "The Basis of Whittier's Critical Creed: The Beauty of the Commonplace and the Truth of Style," *Rice Institute Pamphlet,* XLVII (Oct., 1960), 34–50.

20. *Biog.*, III. 522.

21. *The Complete Poetical Works of Whittier* (Cambridge, Mass., n.d.), The "Cambridge Edition."

### Chapter Eight

1. Willard Thorp, *American Humorists* (Minneapolis, 1964).

2. Eggleston, *op. cit.,* 5.

3. In the character of Frank Archer in his novel *We Accept With Pleasure.* Quoted in Schorer, *op. cit.,* 588.

### Chapter Nine

1. Quoted in Dickey, *Maturity,* 311.

2. Charles A. and Mary R. Beard, *New Basic History of the United States* (New York, 1960), pp. 279–81.

3. Roberts, *op. cit.,* 171.

4. Kreymborg, *op. cit.,* 243.

5. Quoted in Crowder, *op. cit.,* 248.

6. Henry A. Beers, *The Connecticut Wits and Other Essays* (New Haven, 1920), pp. 31–43.

7. This is inaccurate. Garland himself records Riley's experiences of farm work in *Roadside Meetings*, p. 225.

8. Richard A. Cordell, "Limestone, Corn and Literature: The Indiana Scene and its Interpreters," *Saturday Review* (Dec. 17, 1938), pp. 3–4.

9. Leon Edel, review of Robert Frost, *Selected Letters*, ed. by Lawrance Thompson, *Saturday Review* (Sept. 5, 1964).

10. Quoted in Dickey, *Maturity*, 380.

11. Richard Hovey, friend of Bliss Carman, with whom he collaborated in their *Songs from Vagabondia* (1894).

12. Sinclair Lewis, "Editor's Table," *Yale Literary Magazine*, No. 641 (Feb., 1907), 212.

13. Edgar Lee Masters, "James Whitcomb Riley; A Sketch of his Life and an Appraisal of his Work," *The Century*, CXIV (1927), 704–15.

14. Tandy, *op. cit.*, 159.

15. Herron, *op. cit.*, 360.

16. Sinclair Lewis, *Main Street*, Chapter XXII.

# Selected Bibliography

PRIMARY SOURCES

*The Old Swimmin' Hole and 'Leven More Poems*. Cincinnati: George C. Hitt and Co., 1883. (2nd ed. published the same year by Merrill, Meigs and Co., Indianapolis).

*The Boss Girl, A Christmas Story and Other Sketches*. Indianapolis: Merrill, Meigs and Co., 1885. (Published with additional material, as *Sketches in Prose and Occasional Verses*. Indianapolis: Bowen-Merrill Co., 1891).

*Afterwhiles*. Indianapolis: Bowen-Merrill Co., 1887.

*Nye and Riley's Railway Guide*. Chicago: Thompson and Thomas, 1888. Reissued as *Nye and Riley's Wit and Humor* (*Poems and Yarns*), 1900. Written with Edgar Watson (Bill) Nye.

*Old-Fashioned Roses*. London: Longmans and Co., 1888.

*Pipes o' Pan at Zekesbury*. Indianapolis: Bowen-Merrill Co., 1888.

*Rhymes of Childhood*. Indianapolis: Bowen-Merrill Co., 1890.

*Neghborly Poems*. Indianapolis: Bowen-Merrill Co., 1891. A new edition of *The Old Swimmin' Hole* with additional material in verse and prose.

*The Flying Islands of the Night*. Indianapolis: Bowen-Merrill Co., 1891.

*Green Fields and Running Brooks*. Indianapolis: Bowen-Merrill Co., 1892.

*Poems Here at Home*. New York: The Century Co., 1893.

*Armazindy*. Indianapolis: Bowen-Merrill Co., 1894.

*A Child-World*. Indianapolis: Bowen-Merrill Co., 1897.

*Rubaiyat of Doc Sifers*. New York: The Century Co., 1897.

*Home-Folks*. Indianapolis: Bowen-Merrill Co., 1900.

*The Book of Joyous Children*. Indianapolis: Bobbs-Merrill Co., 1902.

*His Pa's Romance*. Indianapolis: Bobbs-Merrill Co., 1903.

*A Defective Santa Claus*. Indianapolis: Bobbs-Merrill Co., 1904.

*Morning*. Indianapolis: Bobbs-Merrill Co., 1907.

*A Hoosier Romance, 1868*. New York: The Century Co., 1910.

This selection from the many volumes published by Riley includes only those volumes which contain a significant amount of new material and excludes those which are substantially reissues of earlier material under new titles. For a detailed account of Riley's complex publishing history, the reader is referred to the invaluable bibliography compiled by A. J. and D. R. Russo.

Collected editions:

*The Lockerbie Book, Containing Poems Not in Dialect.* Indianapolis: Bobbs-Merrill Co., 1911.

*The Hoosier Book, Containing Poems in Dialect.* Indianapolis: Bobbs-Merrill Co., 1916.

Homestead edition. *The Poems and Prose Sketches of James Whitcomb Riley.* 16 vols. New York: Charles Scribner's Sons, 1897–1914.

Greenfield edition. 14 vols. Indianapolis: Bobbs-Merrill Co., 1900–16. A reissue in uniform bindings of selected individual volumes. No collective title.

Biographical edition. *The Complete Works of James Whitcomb Riley.* ed. Edmund H. Eitel. 6 vols. Indianapolis: Bobbs-Merrill Co., 1913. The definitive text; includes a biographical sketch by Eitel. The Memorial edition, 1916, is textually identical.

*The Complete Poetical Works of James Whitcomb Riley.* Indianapolis: Bobbs-Merrill Co., 1937. (Later reprints published by Grosset and Dunlap, New York). The most easily obtainable modern edition; reprints the text of the Biographical edition without the notes.

Letters:

*Letters of James Whitcomb Riley.* ed. William Lyon Phelps. Indianapolis: Bobbs-Merrill Co., 1930.

"Letters of Riley and Bill Nye," by Edmund H. Eitel. *Harper's Magazine,* CXXXVIII (1919).

*Love Letters of the Bachelor Poet, James Whitcomb Riley to Miss Elizabeth Kahle.* Boston, Bibliophile Society, 1922.

SECONDARY SOURCES

1. *Bibliography:*

RUSSO, ANTHONY J. and DOROTHY R. *A Bibliography of James Whitcomb Riley.* Indianapolis: Indiana Historical Society, 1944. Comprehensive information on all of Riley's poetry and prose, including details of first appearance in newspaper or periodical and first in book form for all poems and stories. Full listings of biographical and critical material and selective information on musical settings of the poems.

2. *Biography and criticism:*

ADE, GEORGE. "Riley and his Friends," *Saturday Evening Post* (September 27, 1930), pp. 8–9, 141–46. Riley as the friend of the "very high up and the humble." "Sympathetic fellowship marked his relations with a wide circle of friends, ranging from President Benjamin Harrison to store keepers in Indiana small towns." Includes extracts from letters to literary friends, including Twain, Bliss Carman, Tarkington, Kipling and T. W. Higginson.

BEERS, HENRY A. "The Singer of the Old Swimmin' Hole." *The Connecticut Wits and Other Essays.* New Haven: Yale University Press, 1920. Plea for Riley as "the poet of the American people."

CARMAN, BLISS. *James Whitcomb Riley; An Essay.* New York: privately printed, 1918. An assessment of Riley's character and work based on a friendship of more than twenty years. Riley "never grew old, never grew up"; "a happy sentimentalist, living on in a practical and intellectual age."

CORDELL, RICHARD A. "Limestone, Corn and Literature: The Indiana Scene and its Interpreters," *Saturday Review* (December 17, 1938), pp. 3–4, 14–15. Succinct account of the Indiana literary tradition, deprecating Riley's contribution.

CROWDER, RICHARD. *Those Innocent Years: The Legacy and Inheritance of a Hero of the Victorian Era, James Whitcomb Riley.* Indianapolis: Bobbs-Merrill, 1957. Modern biographical study; supplements Dickey's two volumes with much new material and presents Riley as "the beau ideal of his time and place."

DICKEY, MARCUS. *The Youth of James Whitcomb Riley.* Indianapolis: Bobbs-Merrill, 1919.

————. *The Maturity of James Whitcomb Riley.* Indianapolis: Bobbs-

Merrill, 1922. These two volumes constitute the official biography, based on material supplied by Riley himself and by his nephew and secretary, Edmund H. Eitel.

GARLAND, HAMLIN. *Roadside Meetings.* New York: Macmillan, 1930. Chapter 9, "Vernacular Poets and Novelists," attempts to place Riley in the dialect tradition. Chapter 18, "In Riley's Country," records an interview with Riley at Greenfield, Indiana.

HERRON, IMA H. *The Small Town in American Literature.* New York: Pageant Books, Inc., 1959. (First pub. Durham, N.C.: Duke University Press, 1939). Comprehensive analysis of the various interpretations of small-town life in American literature.

KINDILIEN, CARLIN T. *American Poetry in the Eighteen Nineties: A Study of American Verse, 1890–1899.* Providence, R. I.: Brown University Press, 1956. Chapter I provides an excellent summary of the characteristics of popular and amateur verse of the period; pp. 56–59 the best published short account of Riley's verse, its qualities and defects.

KREYMBORG, ALFRED. *Our Singing Strength: An Outline of American Poetry (1620–1930).* New York: Coward-McCann, 1929. The chapters on "Mid-Western and Far-Western Frontiers" and "The Respectable Democracy" contain useful judgments of a host of minor poets and moralists and sum up the period of the 1870's to 1890's as one of "glib conformity and pallid doubts."

LAUGHLIN, CLARA E. *Reminiscences of James Whitcomb Riley.* New York: Fleming H. Revell, 1916. Sketches of Riley at a conference of the Western Association of Writers and as a man about Indianapolis; notes on his admiration for Stevenson, the early Yeats, Longfellow, Burns, and Dickens.

LEWIS, SINCLAIR. "Editor's Table." *Yale Literary Magazine,* No. 641 (Feb., 1907), p. 212. Editorial panegyric of Riley's poetry.

MASTERS, EDGAR LEE. "James Whitcomb Riley; A Sketch of his Life and an Appraisal of his Work," *Century,* CXIV (1927), 704–15. Appreciative evaluation; presents Riley as the poet of "the rural mirth and innocent sorrows of the County Fair" whose "poems are truer to the current speech of a people than any poems written by an American."

MITCHELL, MINNIE BELLE. *James Whitcomb Riley as I Knew Him.* Greenfield, Ind.: The Old Swimmin' Hole Press, 1949. Biography; emphasis on his early environment by "the last one of a group of early Greenfield friends who knew him well."

MONROE, HARRIET. "James Whitcomb Riley," *Poetry* (Chicago), VIII (September, 1916), 305–07. An obituary editorial; presents Riley as the poet of "the democratic people of the plains."

NICHOLSON, MEREDITH. *The Hoosiers.* New York: Macmillan, 1915. A social history of Indiana, with a useful chapter on its writers.

––––––. "James Whitcomb Riley," *Atlantic Monthly,* CXVIII (1916), 503–14. An obituary article assessing Riley's character, education, reading, and work. Nicholson was an early protégé and close friend of Riley. Revised version of this article was included in Nicholson's *The Man in the Street: Papers on American Topics.* New York: Charles Scribner's Sons, 1921.

––––––. *The Poet.* Boston: Houghton Mifflin, 1914. Sentimental novel in which the chief character (clearly based on Riley) directs the action by benign suggestion and solves all dilemmas by his faith in "romance and poetry."

NOLAN, JEANNETTE COVERT. *James Whitcomb Riley, Hoosier Poet.* New York: Julian Messner, 1941. Biography for juvenile readers.

NOLAN, JEANNETTE COVERT; GREGORY, HORACE; and FARRELL, JAMES T. *Poet of the People: An Evaluation of James Whitcomb Riley.* Bloomington: Indiana University Press, 1951. Contributions to a symposium held at Indiana University in 1949 to commemorate the centenary of Riley's birth.

PARKER, BENJAMIN S. and HEINEY, ENOS B., eds. *Poets and Poetry of Indiana: a representative collection of the poetry of Indiana . . . 1800 to 1900.* New York: Silver, Burdett and Co., 1900. Anthology; selections from the work of 146 poets; includes six poems by Riley. Valuable as an indication of the regional literary enenvironment.

PEARCE, ROY HARVEY. *The Continuity of American Poetry.* Princeton: Princeton Univ. Press, 1961. Chapter 5. "American Renaissance (2): The Poet and the People" contains a valuable analysis of the work of the "Fireside Poets" in creating a mass audience for popular poetry in the late nineteenth century.

PEATTIE, DONALD CULROSS. "Riley as a Nature Poet," *Saturday Review* (July 3, 1937), p. 10. Attempts to present Riley as the "poet of Midwest Nature."

RICHARDS, LOUISE PARK. "James Whitcomb Riley on a Country Newspaper," *Bookman,* XX (1904), pp. 18–24. Records Riley's success as a writer of comic advertising copy for the Anderson *Democrat;* contains an account of the "Leonainie" hoax.

STEGNER, WALLACE. "Western Record and Romance." *Literary History of the United States,* ed. Robert E. Spiller and others. New York: Macmillan, 1948, II, 862–77. Comprehensive summary by Stegner of the interacting strains of realism, romance, sentiment, and dialect humor in the literature of the Middle and Far Western States.

TANDY, JENNETTE *Crackerbox Philosophers in American Humor and Satire*. New York: Columbia University Press, 1925. A valuable study of the tradition of the unlettered philosopher in American humor and satire.

# Index